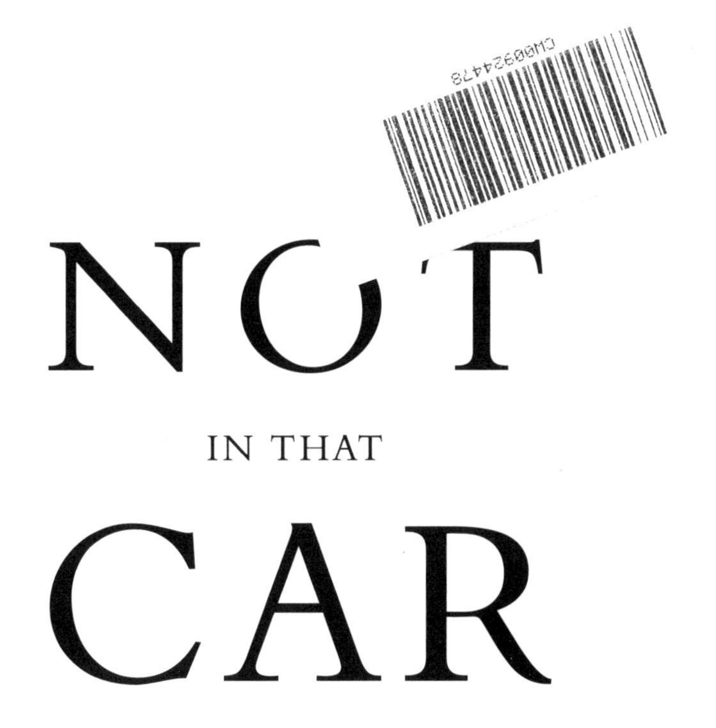



# NOT

## IN THAT

# CAR

A VIEW OF THE WORLD FROM AN

MG MIDGET

# NOT IN THAT CAR

ROY LOCOCK

Matador
5 Weir Road
Kibworth Beauchamp
Leicester LE8 0LQ, UK
Tel: (+44) 116 279 2299
Fax: (+44) 116 279 2277
Email: books@troubador.co.uk
Web: www.troubador.co.uk/matador

ISBN 978 1848766 532

British Library Cataloguing in Publication Data.
A catalogue record for this book is available from the British Library.

Typeset in 11pt Adobe Garamond Pro by Troubador Publishing Ltd, Leicester, UK
Printed and bound in the UK by TJ International, Padstow, Cornwall

**Matador** is an imprint of Troubador Publishing Ltd

*To Bridie*

*still looking after me, love and thanks*

# FORWARD

I knew even before I left Oxford that this adventure would exceed anything else I had experienced in my sixty-one years. It started as a frivolous act emanating from a carelessly phrased and badly timed comment but developed into an epic journey far beyond my blinkered vision.

During the sixteen months that it took to complete I was privileged to touch thousands of lives around the globe, many of them children. In most cases the experience was fleeting, a laugh, a cry of glee or just a smile as we drove past, but if seeing me driving my car, Bridget, caused even one child to develop the ambition to improve his or her life then I shall deem the event a success.

Although officially a solo effort, I was supported throughout by a band of followers, many of whom I have never met, encouraging me via my website, and also the brotherhood that goes to great lengths to maintain the MG marque around the world. I shall be forever grateful to them all.

Quote:
*Bridget has just 3.5" ground clearance under her engine sump. She has enough fuel to drive a maximum of 450 miles, this includes two 20 litre jerry cans. I have a compass and will purchase a map when I enter the different countries, I have also secured 5 days emergency rations should I need to abandon Bridget somewhere in the middle of the wilderness. The only other thing I need is a good psychiatrist.*
Roy Locock

Comment:
*...I am a 27 year old from (Bangalore) India and some day when I*

*can muster enough courage I would like to go on a journey in a manner similar to your adventure. You must have lot of courage and adventure in your heart to do something of this sort, something most of us just fantasize about. I will pray for your safe journey and may you enjoy your amazing adventure.*

Swaroop

# CONTENTS

# CONSPIRACY OF EVENTS

*Location: UK*
*Timeline: February 2006 – June 2008*

Like many of my peers I had always believed, when I gave time to thinking about it, that I would probably die 'in harness' as I loved working. My professional life had been spent mainly in the mobile communications industry – over twenty-two years with the Philips Group of companies, a few years with the mobile phone network O2 and the last thirteen years with my own software and outsourcing company. Then, in late 2005, my wife passed away and I totally lost interest in my work. I decided that if I wasn't enjoying it then I didn't have to do it and so started to dissolve the company.

I had never spent any time considering what I would do when I retired and anyway, I still wasn't sure that I wouldn't go back to work at some stage. Whilst driving home from the office on the penultimate day of the company's trading term I stopped to look at a second-hand car that I had noticed on one or two previous occasions. The car was a 1977 MG Midget, just about old enough to be considered a 'classic'. As a teenager I had always wanted, but couldn't afford, a sports car. Back in those days the MGB was considered the lad's car whilst the Midget was for the girls, but that seemed to have changed as the cars matured and so did the owners.

I decided on impulse to buy the Midget. I hadn't given any serious thought previously to buying it and I realised that I hadn't even given it a serious inspection. I quickly went around all the likely spots where rust would typically occur and lifted the bonnet to peer at the engine.

Not that you can tell much by looking but there were no signs of oil leaks and it appeared generally clean. Just then the proprietor approached and I asked if he had any of the car's historic records. He produced a wallet containing the ownership papers, original warranty document and servicing records for much of its life. I noticed, however, that although the car was built in 1977 it wasn't registered until 1982. The proprietor did not know the reason for this. We finally agreed a price and sealed the deal on the spot. I was now the proud owner of a black 1977 MG Midget 1500 about which I knew very little and anyway, it was years since I had done any kind of work on a motor vehicle.

My first thing to do once I got the car home was to join the MG Owners Club of the UK, which I read about in a document I found in the car. They supplied me with lots of helpful advice on the mechanics, maintenance and care of the car as well as informing me of the differences with other, earlier models.

It was March 2006 and the weather was typical for England at that time of year: cold and wet. I decided it would be nice to get some sunshine and the way to do that would be to take the MG down to Italy. I could drive through France and, as it wasn't too far out of the way, I could include a quick circuit of Spain before crossing the South of France into Italy. This I did, leaving in the June, taking four months to cover a little over six thousands miles and with very little in the way of trouble with the MG. I was so impressed with the way she coped with temperatures in the mid-thirties (centigrade) that I promised her that on our return to England I would undertake a total restoration.

The first challenge that I faced if I was going to give the car a complete make-over was to create enough space in which to be able to work. My garage was typical of the modern day estate dwelling in England, too small in reality to house a car, even one as small as a Midget. So I contacted a builder and had the garage extended. I was obviously going to become a typical classic car owner, spending more on restoring the car than it would ever be worth. Anyway, in August

2007 I started the restoration work in earnest and it was in the middle of that month that I was underneath the Midget struggling to release one of twelve fixing bolts between the engine and the gear box. It was decidedly humid, my legs were suffering from cramp and my fingers were sore from the abrasions caused by tools slipping whilst trying to loosen the nuts with an ill-fitting spanner. Suddenly, a disembodied voice said jovially, "What are you going to do when you've finished restoring this car then, Roy?"

The voice was that of my neighbour and good friend of thirty years, Alan. However, as I hadn't heard him approach I was startled and lifted my torso to see who was there. I cracked my head on the gearbox and heard another voice say, "I'm going to drive the damn thing to Nanjing." I realised then that the second voice was mine. There had been several articles in the recent press about a Chinese company taking over the MG brand and planning to re-start production in Nanjing. My answer was no more than an association of thoughts formed into a sarcastic response to an inopportune question. "Not in that car you can't," he said.

Over the next couple of days the thought of driving to Nanjing kept returning and Alan's response kept resonating around in my head. The idea was definitely starting to appeal and after all, I reasoned, the Midget had behaved well on the drive around Italy, Nanjing was no more than several journeys like that all strung together!

It seems to me that there is something a little unique in the character of some British individuals that rejects judicial thinking; "You can't go to the South Pole, Captain Scott", or "A mile in less than four minutes! You must be crazy Roger", or "Sail around the world single-handed, Mr Chichester? An ill conceived idea if ever I heard one". Of course what is really meant by the critics is that a certain activity hasn't been accomplished before, but, too late, the challenge was made and taken up.

I started browsing the internet during the evenings to find out more about travelling through the various countries that I would need to traverse en route when I discovered the official website of the organisers of the Peking to Paris rally. I called them and spoke to the club secretary. He was most helpful and told me of all the things to be considered on such an adventure, repeatedly emphasising the importance of the car's 'ground clearance'. This concerned me as the Midget has only three and a half inches of clearance beneath the oil sump. Then towards the end of our conversation the secretary asked me what car I was driving and how many were in the party. I told him this was a solo attempt and that I was driving an MG Midget. "You must be bloody crazy!" he said. I reflected for some time on his clear insight into the challenge ahead.

The original idea was still expanding in my head and I more or less decided that to drive all the way to Nanjing just to turn around and return was indeed crazy as people kept telling me. What I should be researching was a right turn at Nanjing, dropping down to Hong Kong and catching a boat over to Australia. From there I could hop over to South America and then drive up through Central America, the USA and finally into Canada where I could ship back to the UK. This sounded far more sensible to me!

Within three weeks of my interchange with Alan on that fateful day in the garage it was decided that the Midget and I were going on an adventure drive somewhere. My research into the first leg from Abingdon (starting from the home of MG) to Nanjing was becoming demoralising as it appeared that the Chinese Government did everything it could to discourage private motorists from visiting their country. Apart from the bureaucracy, they insist that visiting foreigners driving private cars in China must be accompanied by an official guide. The cost of this guide, their transport, food and accommodation has to be borne by the visitor and that was making the costs far too high. They pointed out that the cost for a party of several cars was the same and therefore per individual it became relatively cheaper, but I didn't know several other MG owners crazy enough to join me. Eventually I reluctantly concluded that I really could not justify, even to myself, the disproportionate cost demanded by the Chinese Government. It appeared that the challenge would be left to someone else to pick-up.

For the whole of the winter of 2007 little was done to the car as the temperatures were too low, as was my morale. Then one morning it occurred to me that a circumnavigation of the globe could still be done without entering China. Never mind the factory in Nanjing, there would be other things to see instead. Around the World was going to happen.

It was March 2008 and I researched alternative routes to achieve the goal. My new route would now take me through Turkey, Iran, Pakistan and India. From there I could ship across to Australia and rejoin the original route. I had researched the idea of crossing from India through Burma (Myanmar) and into Thailand, Malaysia and Singapore but the Burmese regime quickly knocked that idea on the head. After all, an old man driving an old car might easily cause massive civil disturbance and bring down the military government!

The restoration was progressing slowly when another neighbour offered to help me restore the seats in the car but on condition that we did them immediately. He had been in the upholstery industry for many years, so his expertise was exactly what I needed. It transpired that we had to do them straight away because he and his wife had decided to emigrate to Australia within weeks, so we would not have another chance. I discussed with Mike my planned trip and he was very polite but I could tell from his reaction that he belonged to the group that thought I was crazy. However, he said, "Well if you make it to Oz, you must promise to visit us."

I suddenly realised that time was passing by with little real progress regarding the adventure so I decided, and announced, that I would be leaving around the end of May. This was a purely artificial date just to ensure that things started to happen and I quickly realised what a mountain of tasks I had to accomplish to meet this deadline. This produced more and more doubters of the scheme, which in turn increased my determination to do it.

The restoration actually consisted of stripping the car down to its bare shell, re-spraying it to change the original black finish to Brooklands Green, replacing the entire interior trim and hood, refurbishing the seats, a half re-build of the engine and replacement of the clutch plate. The engine half rebuild turned out to be a mistake and I really don't remember why I didn't check the pistons, rings and big ends, or refurbish the carburettors. These mistakes were to cost me later and could have had fatal consequences for the journey.

The major part of the restoration work was complete by mid-May although work on the engine went on up until three days before my departure. The final departure date was set for 23rd June 2008 and so that there would be no last minute delays I purchased a ticket for the channel tunnel train to take me across to France. I obtained tourist visas for Iran, Pakistan, India and Australia, and also purchased road maps for all of them except Australia, which I thought I would get on arrival, and Iran, which I couldn't find a copy of anywhere. In fact I eventually sourced an Iranian road map from a very good bookshop in Vienna. Many people suggested taking a GPS navigating system with me but I felt that it was cheating, and anyway, finding complete countries each time couldn't really be that difficult, could it?

Two days before departure I capitulated on one modification to the car that had been recommended and that was the fitting of a sump guard. This was, in fact, the only non-standard modification that I did. Everything else was factory standard and I was just going to have to allow for the lack of ground clearance that, with the sump guard, was now down to under three inches.

The boot of the car was taken up with spare parts, axle stands, tools, car jack and spare wheel. The only non-vehicle item in there was my laptop computer. I had fitted a luggage rack to the boot that had two twenty litre jerry cans strapped to it for carrying spare fuel. The car's hard-top would stay at home as I was 'following the sun'. Behind the car's seats were my emergency shelter, sleeping bag, cold weather clothing (emergencies only), survival equipment and emergency rations. In the passenger foot-well were trainers and walking boots, and the passenger seat held two sports bags of clothing. With the soft-top up it was snug, but the cat would have to swing elseware!

I also had a briefcase containing all my original documentation, electronic copies of which I also kept on my laptop and hardcopies in a separate bag. I had a Carnet for the MG, which is similar to a passport for a vehicle and avoids having to import and export it in every country. My only concern about the car, at that time, was with regards to Iran, the car's registration number being SPY 122X!

During the preparation period I received tremendous support from everyone around me, even though most thought it was crazy. I never have known if my immediate family thought I would do it, but they gave me the unconditional support that they always do. My girlfriend was the one individual that had no doubts as to my ability to accomplish the trip but was completely against the whole idea as she felt I was unnecessarily putting my life in harm's way. We hardly spoke for three months.

I had also decided during the lead up to the departure date that the adventure should have a more important purpose than just satisfying my personal needs, and so I contacted UNICEF and we agreed to use the event to raise funds in support of their work. To help in this aspect I felt we should have a website tracking my progress and to act as a diary recording the adventure, and my financial advisors, Financial Private Clients, offered the services of their IT specialists to set up and maintain this for me, at their cost.

A small departure ceremony was arranged, to take place outside what had been the administrative headquarters of Morris Garages (which is where the brand MG comes from), but is today the Law

Courts in Oxford. Permission to hold the event was granted by Oxfordshire County Council, Oxford City Council and the Thames Valley Police, but unfortunately the police headquarters forgot to tell the officers at the Oxford Police Station opposite the Law Courts. So when I turned up in my MG with two twenty litre jerry cans of petrol strapped to the back of the car and proceeded to reverse right up to the doors of the Law Courts, local plod became a little perplexed. However, Alan, who had become the mission controller, soon sorted out the communications problem and we were allowed to proceed. The official event took place on Sunday 22nd June 2008 and then I nipped home for the night with the intention of making an early start on the Monday morning.

# NINE DAYS ACROSS EUROPE

*Location: Europe and Turkey*
*Timeline: 23rd June 2008 – 22nd July 2008*

Well, the first week of the journey was a little like the curate's egg (and I employ the term in its modern usage), good in parts, which I guessed would be the pattern of things for the future.

Apart from the anticipation of what might lie ahead there was really little excitement as we sped through Europe to get to places I hadn't seen before and which are culturally very different from home.

From the Channel Tunnel our route took us past Brugges, Brussels and Liege in Belgium until we arrived in Spa, where we spent the first night. During this opening day of the journey the car suffered the first mechanical problem before reaching Folkestone, with the gear knob falling off (clearly the result of poor workmanship). This was re-attached during our incarceration in the Channel Tunnel.

Prior to leaving on the second day I removed the valve rocker cover and checked that the head nuts were tight, having covered fifteen hundred miles since the engine rebuild, and whilst I was at it I also checked the valve clearances. The car was only completed a week before we left. Even though I have a good understanding of how engines work, I am not a mechanic, and without the verbal encouragement from Alan badgering me on, I found I was a little nervous about doing anything to the engine. Long consultations with the handbook preceded any action under the bonnet which made me angry with myself for my lack of confidence, but then again, without any roadside assistance available I was feeling vulnerable.

Then on into Germany, which was one European country I hadn't seen before, but many of the names were familiar: Mannheim, Nuremberg, and Regensburg. This was slightly different to the projected route, which would have taken us further south, but was in fact more direct than it looked on the map. Everything was running well except that when Bridget's engine had been running for more than an hour it had a tendency to stall if I stopped for traffic. Then on day three, for no apparent reason, it decided to eject most of the engine coolant all over a service area forecourt. I was at the rear of the car refuelling when I looked down and saw a growing puddle of liquid. Initially fearing it to be petrol I stopped the pump, but quickly realised that it was in fact coolant. I retired for a cup of coffee and after Bridget's engine had cooled down for an hour, I topped up the level. I have never yet found out what caused Bridget to eject the coolant and there has never been a repetition of the problem. A minor adjustment to the carburettors cleared the stalling problem but she then suffered from a slight over-run when I switched off the ignition. I would just have to keep 'twiddling'!

From Germany we crossed the border into Austria where I headed for Vienna. Although I had visited the city before, it held fond memories for me and so I had decided that I wanted to spend a couple of days there. However, when I arrived every hotel I came across was full. Nobody had told me, but there was a football match between Spain and Russia, the semi-finals of the European 2008 Championships, being played in the city that evening. As a rule I don't book hotels in advance as trying to find a specific address is often more difficult than just stopping at the first hotel you come across, but on this occasion it would have been useful. I couldn't find anything available anywhere in the city.

Having enquired at more than a dozen hotels I was about to give up trying to find accommodation when I spied the Best Western Reither Hotel. I quickly established that they had no vacant rooms and was about to leave when the owners approached me. Mr & Mrs Reither were told by the receptionist of my plight and, having spied Bridget parked outside, asked me about her and what I was doing in Vienna. When I explained they immediately offered me accommodation at an apartment they owned in the city and made me very welcome. Their hospitality was excellent and they went out of their way to make me comfortable.

I had a day's rest from driving and enjoyed the beauty of Vienna, even with the thousands of football fans milling about singing football songs and chanting slogans. Leaving on the Saturday morning I headed for Budapest in Hungary. Budapest is really two cities in one, with Buda, the hilly part to the west, and Pest, the flat area in the east, divided by the river Danube. The iconic Lion Bridge across the river is identical in design to the bridge over the River Thames at Marlow, although somewhat bigger.

The first one thousand miles was now behind us, and only thirty-eight more (thousands that is) to go. Bridget was holding up well given the fairly high temperatures (thirty-five degrees centigrade) and hour after hour of steady driving for several days in succession. Cars of Bridget's vintage were not designed for this type of motoring as there were few motorways around in those days.

I struck out for Bucharest, stopping overnight in Brad. The condition of the roads noticeably deteriorated once we had crossed the border into Romania. The majority of roads were now single carriageway and the road surfaces were often furrowed by eight inch ruts carved by forty-four tonne trucks as they ploughed through the hot soft tarmac. One particular detour we were sent on, whilst repairs were being carried out to the main highway, took us past a town called Deva. The route ostensibly was made up of a number of cart tracks joined up by what appeared to be a concrete runway, and where each part was joined there were sizeable steps. Bridget's new sump guard was utilised for the first time.

Romania is a country of contrasts, with large areas of very flat landscape, similar to Norfolk in the UK, and then stunning mountainous regions such as the Southern Carpathians and the Balkans within a hundred miles of Bucharest, the capital.

Bridget was commanding a lot of interest everywhere now and I became accustomed to cars cruising alongside whilst passengers, and even occasionally the driver, took photographs, usually with their mobile phones. It wasn't only the men that found Bridget interesting either, many women smiled and waved and in one instance I thought a group of squealing women were even going to start throwing underwear, but after half an hour of waiting I gave up and went on my way. It appears that many of the ladies found Bridget's size appealing as on more than one occasion they would point and say, in English, 'little'; at least I think it was Bridget they were referring to!

The following week Bridget was a little poorly. With the engine run-on mentioned earlier and a newly appeared oil leak from her offside (UK) rear wheel I decided to pop into a garage in Bucharest and get her fixed up (frankly I didn't think the hotel I stayed at would appreciate good British axle oil on the forecourt). The staff at the garage were very warm, friendly and enthusiastic; it should have served as a warning. At one stage eight mechanics were attempting to make her feel better. Unfortunately their enthusiasm was greater than their ability and after eight and a half hours her engine was back to how it was when we arrived, having been in far more serious straights at various times of the day. At least the oil leak was fixed with a ring seal and gasket from *my* spares store!

After staying two nights in Bucharest I moved on towards Turkey by way of Bulgaria. Bridget was back to her best after a little adjustment, cruising almost effortlessly through the Bulgarian countryside. The road surfaces appeared to have improved compared to Romania, but be warned, if you do drive there, watch out for the unexpected potholes; these do tend to be teeth rattling should you get caught unaware. Also, should you see roadside signs warning of speed radar, take them at face value. Speed traps, sorry, safety monitors are far more common than the UK. Map reading can also be difficult as most of the towns have a European name, usually shown on the map, and a local name, normally shown on signposts. Sometimes both are shown. I am not sure if the local name is written in Bulgarian or Russian, but there are characters not used in other European alphabets and they are mixed with numbers.

The scenery of Bulgaria is considerably different to Romania with many of the main roads lined with a wide variety of trees (none of which I can name), making a pleasant change from the pines that are so common across much of Europe. We crossed the Balkan mountain range in the centre of Bulgaria; they are beautiful, but the roads are largely single carriageway and through the mountains the heavy goods vehicles make things a little tedious. I decided to spend Wednesday night in Stara Zagora (Стара Загора as it is spelt in Bulgarian or possibly Russian) as it was the nearest reasonable sized town to the Turkish border. On arrival I took the opportunity to treat Bridget to a wash and brush up; she deserved it.

The following morning Bridget needed petrol so we pulled into a Bulgarian service station. Earlier I noticed a car that had passed us, then dropped back behind us and proceeded to tail us for several miles. This car pulled in to the same service station just after us and a man jumped out and came running over. He was holding out a packet of biscuits and said, “I work for a confectionary company that makes biscuits and I would like to give you these as a present. It is a beautiful car.” I was quite taken aback, firstly because his English was so good, and secondly that a guy should be so moved at seeing any sort of car that he would bother to do this, but this would not be the only instance.

As we crossed the border from Bulgaria into Turkey we were approached by a customs officer on the Bulgarian side. He was quite young, exceptionally well turned out in his uniform, which is a little unusual for customs officers, who normally have their tie under one ear and their breakfast down their jacket, and he wore a very stern expression. My immediate reaction was "Oh God what have I done wrong?" He approached the car and, bending down to look me in the eye, he said, "Mr Bond, James Bond?" With that, his expression broke into a huge smile. Clearly he had noticed the licence plate on his closed circuit television and we shared the joke, but it made me wonder if the officials on the Iranian border would be so amused.

It was my intention to make Istanbul our first overnight stay in Turkey. The road conditions were good, traffic was light and the sun was very warm. I had probably not driven more than forty miles when on rounding a bend, I saw a large rock on the road, about one hundred and fifty metres ahead. There was nothing travelling towards me and I checked my mirrors to make sure that nobody was behind me in preparation to pull out into the middle of the road, thus avoiding the rock. When my eyes returned to the obstruction it appeared to have moved from the left-hand side of my half of the road and was now in the centre of my traffic lane! However, my brain was saying to me, "Something is wrong, rocks cannot move unaided." I started braking and then to my astonishment saw the rock move forward again to the centre of the road. Bridget and I were now within thirty metres of it as we came to a halt and now I could see that it wasn't a rock at all, but a very large tortoise. I quickly put on Bridget's hazard lights, checked that there was still no other traffic and got out of the MG. I escorted the tortoise, which took no notice of me whatsoever, to the far side of the road before returning to my car and continuing down the road. I wondered how common a sight that was but didn't see any others myself.

From a mechanical viewpoint the day's journey was quite uneventful but we passed the two thousand mile point. Bridget was still running well and I intended to stay for a couple of days and give her a rest. However, I really didn't gel with Istanbul for some unexplainable reason and so decided to drive on again. According to the itinerary we were supposed to go straight to Ankara but I rather fancied heading down past the Gallipoli Peninsula and towards the Mediterranean. We made it without incident to Izmir, some five hundred miles on and the furthest Bridget had ever been from home.

I thought we would stay at Izmir for a couple of days. Bridget had her 'top off ' for the first time (I had been apprehensive about being able to put it up again as the new seals make it very difficult) and I managed to get both arms and face sunburnt. I determined to take a tour of Ephesus the next day whilst Bridget had a well deserved rest. She had made it past the two thousand five hundred mile mark in less than twelve days, which I thought was pretty good going. The drive was quite tiring, particularly leaving Istanbul. Bridget attracted so much attention that I was literally waving to cars on the right and left as they honked their horns or just waved. The thought did occur to me that if I was waving to both sides, who was steering? I was seriously concerned at one stage when I looked in the rear-view mirror and saw cars jostling for position behind me. I really thought that our presence could cause an accident, but fortunately all passed well. However, it did increase the concentration required and I was also very conscious of constantly scanning the dials, checking coolant temperature, oil pressure, etc.

Week three started with me on strike. We were some four hundred miles off course, north of Marmaris, on the south-west coast of Turkey. On rounding a bend at the top of a mountain range we were presented with a beautiful panorama consisting of a small bay skirted by fir trees and a small sandy beach. After two weeks driving I decided that was where I was going to stay for at least the next two and a half days.

At the edge of the sea was the village of Gokova, a local holiday resort and traditional fishing village. The place had plenty of hotels and I found accommodation without difficulty. The whole place was very relaxing, the sun shone for ten hours a day, and the sea was clean and warm.

Reinvigorated by the relaxed atmosphere of Gokova we got back on the road Wednesday morning. By late afternoon we had covered just over four hundred miles and were back on course in Ankara. There was heightened security around the city following a terrorist attack on the American Consulate in Istanbul but apart from extra roadside checks there was nothing to bother us. Then, the day following the attack in Istanbul, three German tourists on a climbing holiday on Mount Ararat, in the east of the country, were kidnapped by the PKK group and two police officers were killed near the Iranian border when their vehicle was destroyed by a landmine. As this was the direction we were headed I realised that we could have some interesting times during the next week.

After a brief one day stopover we were back on the road to a small Black Sea resort called Ordu. It was my intention to stay for three days and move again on Tuesday.

Bridget was still running well generally but began stalling, again, once her engine was hot. There was also the hint of a backfire under heavy load and some of the mountain roads did make the going tough in the forty degree heat. By now I thought I knew the car pretty well but it does take a little time to get to know what to expect under different conditions. Initially I was very nervous of the temperature her engine was running at, just because the indicator was different to how it used to be before the rebuild.

It was a difficult trip from Ankara to Ordu, firstly because it rained (first time on this journey), making the road surfaces treacherous, and secondly because for two stretches, of around ten kilometres each, the road had been stripped of the top three layers and was little more than a hard gravel track. Although we only grounded once (thanks due again to the sump guard for doing its job) the vibration was so bad at times that things were becoming loose and the normal rattles were increasing. I had to take time out to give her a thorough check.

Well, after five days, Ordu was finally put behind us. We took the coast road to Trabzon, a distance of no more than one hundred and twenty miles. The scenery was pleasant but not spectacular, much the same as many other coast roads in European countries such as Spain or Italy. The traffic was its usual horn tooting, waving, jostling self and the day was shaping up to be a generally relaxed affair. Arriving on the outskirts of Trabzon at around eleven o'clock, I noticed that one particular vehicle that had been trailing me for a little distance now moved up on the outside of Bridget. I looked over and the driver made it clear that he would like to stop and chat.

Since I had plenty of time on my hands and we were on the edge of town I thought, why not, so I let him overtake and a couple of hundred metres up the road we stopped. He jumped out of his vehicle and started back towards me, checked, went back to his vehicle and got something from the passenger side and again started towards me. He was carrying a small can, similar in size and shape to a sixteen pint party can of lager. He smiled and proffered it to me, at the same time clearly speaking about Bridget. I could make out "welcome" and "beautiful" amongst other words and it became obvious that it was a re-run of the chap in Bulgaria that gave me the biscuits. This time the can, unfortunately not containing ice cold lager, was full of olives, to which I am particularly partial. It was a wonderful gesture that made me feel quite touched. I just can't imagine anyone in the UK ever doing that for a stranger to the country, no matter what they were driving.

It is always a challenge, on arriving at a new destination, to find accommodation, and Trabzon was no different. It is true you often see parts of the city that you might not otherwise see, but that's not always a good thing. With Trabzon I eventually gave up and stopped a passing pedestrian, making it clear that I was hopelessly lost. He studied my map for a few moments and gave me directions in broken English and gestures. I had to take a right turn, followed by another, then at the square I had to go left. I set off, but after the second right-hand turn it didn't look correct for some reason so I pulled over to look at the map again. Then the man that had given me directions suddenly appeared at the window. He realised that the first turn I took was the wrong one and figured out where I would end up, so had dashed through some pedestrian shortcuts to re-emerge just as I stopped. Again it demonstrated the helpfulness of the people in Turkey and the lengths they are prepared to go even for strangers.

I had arranged for a package, containing specially created postcards of Bridget and a crucial cable that I required for the camcorder, to be sent via a courier service to the hotel. It was due to arrive on Friday but it so happened that the same day I was intending to visit the Sümela monastery, a short distance away. I got the hotel to check when the package would be delivered, thinking I would arrange my visit so as not to clash with the delivery. We had promised the courier a photo shoot of the delivery. By good luck and excellent service the package was in fact a day early and would be delivered just two hours after my arrival. The photo shoot turned into a rugby scrum as many of the locals thought that they could get in on it and good humoured chaos reigned.

Saturday 19th July and we had made our way, only just, to Erzurum, en route to the Iranian border. The journey was at times spectacular and at others merely very pleasant. The scenery, particularly in the mountain ranges, is absolutely beautiful. I was very proud of the way in which Bridget took it all in her stride as at times the climbs were very severe. I should have realised of course that 'pride comes before a fall' and sure enough when we reached the town centre the engine was sounding really sick. She stalled several times and when just three hundred metres short of the hotel Bridget all but gave up. I thought for a moment that I would have to walk those last few metres but with one last gasp the engine produced just enough power to make it. Certainly the approach was quite steep but it shouldn't have been a problem. I spent a couple of hours checking plugs, liquid levels and adjusting the points. By the time I finished she was starting up alright so I thought I would leave it and see how things went the next day.

Trying to plan ahead for once, I had come to the conclusion that hotels in Iran did not have internet, because I had been trying to make a reservation but none of those advertised had email addresses available. I was beginning to suspect that the web was a forbidden facility, in which case I was afraid my reports would dry up for around three weeks. I told Mission Control I would do my best to keep them in the picture and I was sure they would post titbits when they got them.

It was whilst trawling the net that I came across a small item on a blog warning that visitors to Iran required hard currency as credit cards, travellers cheques, etc. were not accepted, even at banks. Trying not to panic I checked with a number of travel sites and this confirmed my worst fears. I had to find a source of US dollars, pounds sterling or Euros, and quickly. By good fortune the concierge at the hotel knew of an ATM that dispensed US dollars as well as Turkish Lire, a rare but useful facility. I withdrew my maximum amount two days in a row and hoped that I would be able to do so at our next destination. Although not as much as I would normally want, it should suffice if I was frugal.

The following day we only had about one hundred and eighty miles to travel, which was good as Bridget was still suffering and it would give me time to find another dollar ATM.

I managed, again, to get my face burnt by the sun. I had the roof down but it was cloudy for the first part of the journey. However, once we cleared the peak of the mountain range the sun came out and I donned my bandana to save the top of my head from frying, as most of its natural protection fell out a long time previously. The sun did not feel particularly strong but it must have been. I was wondering if the Americans might detect a new source of radiation in Iran on the Tuesday and start another diplomatic incident!

It was Monday 21st July and we were in Dogubayazit on what was to be my last full day in Turkey. After having worked out in the gym at Erzurum (first time for over seven weeks) and found my fitness level wanting, I decided that I would walk from the hotel to Ishak Pasha Sarayi, some ten kilometres distant. It is a palace that was built in the seventeenth century and is only fifteen kilometres from Mount Ararat.

History records that the Pasha (a local governor) was so pleased with the design of the palace that he had the architect's hands chopped off so that he couldn't design a better one for anyone else. A little drastic you might think but I was wondering if we could do something similar in the UK but with estate agents.

A short distance from the palace was another building and some interesting rock formations and caves above it. I decided to do my impression of a Turkish mountain goat and climbed to the summit from where the view was terrific. Then I spied three guys doing similar things not far away and because of the recent kidnappings I was somewhat wary. This was not, after all, a busy tourist area. As I made my way down from the summit they were ascending and so sooner or later our paths would cross. Rounding a large boulder there they were and they turned and spoke in perfect Turkish, I think! Trying to look totally relaxed I smiled and said, "Hello", which caused them to look at each other quizzically. Anyway, they indicated that they wanted me to take a photograph of them posing on a rock ledge and things went from there. They wanted to know where I was from and told me that they were with the Turkish army. They soon became friendly and took many photos as well as buying me lunch. At the end of the day they had to return to barracks but we had all enjoyed a very warm and pleasant time trying to make ourselves understood to each other. There are few barriers that cannot be broken down if the will is there.

# AXIS OF EVIL

*Location: Iran*
*Timeline: 22nd July 2008 – 6th August 2008*

On arriving at the border post into Iran I was a little nervous. There was no smart uniformed customs official this time but a man in civilian clothes approached and asked if he could help. Having no idea how the system of entering the country worked here, and being a little apprehensive about how I would be received, I asked the chap where tourists had to go to complete the immigration procedures. He was wearing an ID tag around his neck and, looking 'official', proceeded to tell me which buildings I had to go to and the function of each part of the process, as well as which documents I would need to present. He turned out to be a 'Mr Fixit', one of a band of guys that hang around most border posts where there are a lot of people crossing and the administration is complex. They assist in return for some sort of reward, in this case he merely wanted me to buy some currency from him instead of the official Exchange Bureau. This was the only time I used this type of unofficial arrangement at a border as I found that in most cases the officials would tell you what you needed and where to go to complete it.

I had established before arriving that anyone entering Iran with a foreign registered car who intended staying more than fifteen days is supposed to put temporary Iranian licence plates on their vehicle. However the official that dealt with me wrote a lengthy letter which he gave to me and said, "If anyone stops you and asks about your registration give them this letter and it will be OK."

The UK Government's official travel advice with regard to Iran includes "avoid large gatherings or protests". Such manoeuvres can be very difficult if you are the reason for the gathering and the crowd comes to you. On entering Iran I had to park Bridget, whilst going off to collect insurance documents. I was approximately twenty yards inside the country's boundary and very nearly caused a riot (one for the Guiness Book of Records). I parked behind a lorry and in front of a taxi, where the customs official had told me to. Within three minutes there must have been at least thirty males of varying ages all jostling to see and touch Bridget, and traffic was stopping so the drivers could see and take photos. One driver, however, wasn't interested and tried in vain to get out of the line of vehicles, ending up blocking the road just as a police car arrived. Lots of whistle blasts were heard and the officer shouted something at the unfortunate man that was trying to get on with his business. The driver took exception to the officers' comments and jumped from his vehicle ready to square up to the traffic cop. Just then a second police car arrived and luckily diffused the situation by weight of numbers but for a few moments it looked like things could have got out of hand. Anyway, the driver left and all the men returned to milling around and discussing Bridget.

The drive from the border to Tabriz, my first stop-over, was uneventful, though the Iranian traffic is a little more erratic than even the Turks. You also have to be very careful in towns because the Iranians will stop at the side of the road and throw open their doors without thought of other vehicles.

The terrain in Iran is far more barren than Turkey and the mountain ranges craggy. We spent three days in Tabriz and experienced the first real taste of Persian hospitality and their culture. The warmth of the people is every bit as sincere as the Turks and they are very curious about foreigners. I was continually approached in the streets by people who wanted to talk to me, even when all they knew of the English language was to say, "Hello, how are you. You are welcome here." I met a fellow guest, an Iranian staying at the hotel with his wife and two work colleagues, and spoke briefly about what I was doing. Later, around six o'clock, I saw them again and he sent his party off in a taxi to the bazaar saying that he would like to walk with me if I didn't mind. We walked and talked for almost two hours when his mobile phone rang. Suddenly he was very apologetic and said he had to return to the hotel because he had forgotten that he was due to take his wife to a friend's house for dinner. We eventually arrived back half an hour late.

Clearly I was wrong about Iran not having internet facilities and it is both very common and heavily used. I have no idea why adverts for the hotels did not carry their e mail addresses.

On Thursday I decided to visit a village called Kandovan, around sixty-five kilometres south of Tabriz. All the houses are carved out of volcanic lava that has formed hive shaped mounds similar to, but larger than, termite hills. I was talking to another guest, this time an Iranian who had lived in the States for several years, and he enquired of the staff about the cost of a taxi for me. The next thing I knew was that two of the staff, one who had a car and the other who spoke reasonable English, had volunteered to take me to Kandovan as it was their day off. That sort of hospitality I found everywhere during my first few days in Iran.

Friday 25th July and we were back on the road, this time to Astara on the coast of the Caspian Sea. Bridget started off sounding and running a little rough but after about forty miles seemed to settle down into her rhythm and I relaxed too. We were stopped at checkpoints no less than five times by the police during the journey, which was annoying most of the time but turned out to be a good thing on one occasion after I had taken an unscheduled diversion (wrong turn). It transpired that I was heading into Azerbaijan on a road that was not an authorised crossing or on my route! What was that I was saying earlier – finding a complete country shouldn't be difficult?

The journey between Ardabil and Astara was simply unbelievable.

Bridget had been attracting all the usual attention from other road users although perhaps with a little more hustling, when we came to a long queue of traffic caused by an accident. Being Friday it was the start of the Iranian's weekend and the traffic was very heavy compared to normal weekdays. Anyway, we had cars literally all around us, some even using the hard shoulder, then people started getting out of their cars and taking photos of Bridget, coming up to talk to me and offering me sweets and fruit. I was surprised just how widely spoken English is in Iran, even the children speaking it. Family picnics are a big thing in Iran and Turkey, and many of the people were on their way to their favourite spots. The traffic moved a little and then stopped again and the crowding would start all over. After about forty-five minutes the traffic started to move again, but slowly, and we were going down a mountain road still three abreast. I looked across to see who was on the outside of me and there were three guys and a girl in the car. Their car window was down and after chatting for a few minutes they invited me to join them for a picnic lunch. So a few hundred metres further on we stopped at a parking area and had a very pleasant meal and chat, and of course took lots of photos.

An incident when I arrived at Astara later in the day reinforced two things for me that were useful reminders of security when travelling in unfamiliar countries. We were driving into the outskirts of the town when I pulled over to ask where I could find a good hotel. Immediately there were three men looking over the car and talking in a curious but friendly fashion about the car and my journey. Then I was ushered over to the rear of a car parked just in front of Bridget, the boot was opened and before I knew it I was being offered a drink of illicit local brandy! I politely refused for two reasons, the first being that I was driving and had no idea how strong the alcohol might be, and secondly because the punishment for a European caught drinking alcohol in Iran might well be severe depending on the political climate at the time. I thanked my unexpected hosts and drove a little further down the road.

Then I spied two young lads on motor scooters talking at the side of the road and again asked for directions. They said to follow them into town and they would show me the location of a good hotel. Not to my surprise, as we drove through the market and the town centre there was lots of whistling and shouts from people who clearly knew the guys escorting me and we also collected several more scooter mounted lads.

After ten minutes of this and some hesitant turns into smaller streets I started to become suspicious of where these lads were leading me. Eventually they pulled up outside a fairly dilapidated building that I was pretty sure was not a hotel, so rather than risk getting out of the car I called to them, saying that I wanted a "good European style hotel", and started to pull away. They did their best to stop me but were unable to do so until I came up to some traffic lights several streets away. There they caught up and started hooting their horns and shouting. As the lights turned to green I started to pull away when a big Mercedes passed me and stopped. Although a little nervous I had no option but to stop and the Mercedes driver got out of his car, at the same time saying something to the leader of the lads. They immediately melted away with just a final defiant honk on their horns and the Mercedes driver approached Bridget. He asked if he could help and I told him I was looking for a hotel. He replied that if I would like to follow him he would take me to the hotel that he was staying at, although he would understand if I preferred to find my own way. The hotel he guided me to was excellent and it transpired that he was an Iranian business man based in the UK who imported marble from the Astara area and was just visiting for a few days. With hindsight I believe the lads were just high spirited and meant no real harm, but it served as a reminder that when entering an unfamiliar town or city you can never be too sure what the neighbourhood you are in is like.

Saturday and I went to the local beach. Segregated bathing, and all signs in Persian, make for a potentially hazardous guessing game. But once again my guardian angel was watching over me and a passing lifeguard, seeing that I was unsure, took me under his wing and showed me where to go. He also fed me and took the opportunity to practise his English. At the end of the afternoon he invited me to go to his home, which he shared with another lifeguard, and have some tea. The house consisted of a single room, bare walls and stone floors, with a minimum of furniture. There was a small kitchen area in one corner of the room and two beds at the far end. Functional, but it made me realise how fortunate we are in Western Europe.

When I returned to the hotel I spent a promised couple of hours trying to tune Bridget's engine. After a slight adjustment to the timing she was running better, but the 'running on' was still bad. Just have to keep trying!

It had been a fascinating start to my visit to the Peoples Republic of Iran and I was looking forward to the rest of it. I was also going to have to spend more time working on Bridget, paying special attention to the timing.

From Astara we ventured along the coast road to Rasht and then down to Tehran. Again we attracted the attention of the local plod, this time in the guise of motorway police. They pulled us over for a good look at the car but couldn't even guide us to a decent hotel.

After driving around the major routes of Tehran for about an hour I stopped to study the map and try to figure out whereabouts we were in relation to the city. Suddenly there was a whoop of joy and two lads on a motorcycle stopped alongside me. We chatted for several minutes and I asked them if they could give me directions. They said that they could do better than that and told me to follow them. I had this feeling of deja vu. After about fifteen minutes of weaving through Tehran traffic, and that's a feat not to be underestimated, we arrived at a great hotel. The lads wouldn't accept anything for their trouble except one of Bridget's postcards each.

On the second day in Tehran I realised that I was fast running out of US Dollars. I had already established that travellers cheques and debit/credit cards were not accepted anywhere in Iran, but I thought in the capital it might be different. A quick call to the British Embassy soon settled it as they confirmed that neither method of payment would be accepted, only hard currency: US Dollars, Euros or GB Pounds. They said they could get me some money from the UK but it would take around ten days. When I said I didn't have enough money to stay for that time they just said, "Get out then." So I decided I would have to budget tightly and make a dash for the border. It was going to mean pushing Bridget a little harder than I had wanted before arriving at the Pakistan border, but needs must.

From Tehran I drove down to Esfahan, some three hundred miles south. Although Bridget's engine did not sound too good at the end, she coped very well. We ran out of petrol some fifty miles short of our destination. Iran is the third largest producer of oil in the world and yet there are vast distances between filling stations and people often have to queue for fuel. I passed queues of lorries as long as three quarters of a mile at some locations. They also have a ration scheme whereby they are allocated a number of litres of very cheap (less than ten pence a litre) fuel each month and use a chip and pin card in a similar way to a mobile phone pay-as-you-go card. Once they have used their allocation they have to pay around twenty-five pence per litre.

Anyway, as I said, Bridget ran out of fuel and so I used one of the jerry cans for the first time. As usual, although in a lay-by on a major route, a small number of people gathered to take photos and just as I was about to leave a car pulled up and asked one of the onlookers how far it was to the next service area. From his reaction he clearly wasn't going to make it so I gave him some fuel from one of the cans; it was as if I had handed him a bar of gold, he was that grateful.

Well, we arrived in Esfahan with temperatures in the mid forties degree centigrade and Bridget needed a rest, so we took a day off. I decided to walk around the town to see what might be of interest. Iran is big on mosques in the same way Italy is with Duomos, so I was hoping for something different. I found a building that looked similar but in some way different to the normal mosque and decided to make a closer inspection. It turned out to be a famous (in the Muslim world) school of theology called Chaharbagh. Its architecture, decoration and setting are really beautiful. As I was about to leave I was approached by a man in uniform who said, "Hello, welcome to Esfahan. What country are you from?" So I told him and we spoke for several minutes, during which I noticed an emblem on his shoulder and the word Police. His English was very good so I asked him what department of the police he was in. He replied proudly, "I am with the Tourist Police." Without thinking I pointed to his gun and said, "And is that for shooting bad tourists?" Fortunately he realised that it was my off-beat sense of humour and laughed politely. We were joined by another man who wanted to ask some questions and it turned out that he was a Mullah who taught at the school. I was invited to tea (which they drink all day long) with him in his 'cell' and he offered to be my guide for the rest off the day. Now being from Oxford I know what a professor's 'cell' is like: eight bedrooms, six bathrooms, etc. However, this man's cell was twelve feet by ten with one end curtained off for his bed and robes. The remainder was plain walls, cushions on the floor and book shelves all around the room. Once we had finished our tea he couldn't wait to change out of his robes and into his civilian gear, get out his 125cc motorbike (which appears to be compulsory for every resident of the country) and show me around his city.

We spent the remainder of the day sightseeing, and in discussion about pretty much everything, including politics and religion. There was one interlude in a bazaar, whilst we were talking, a couple stopped us and the lady said, "I saw you on the road yesterday in that beautiful car." This was followed within two minutes by another couple approaching us and asking if they could have their photo taken with me. They had never set eyes on me before, nor I them; the whole episode was quite surreal.

The first day of August and we were back on the road completing over five thousands miles since the start of our adventure. Another first, we were stopped for speeding! I honestly had no idea what the speed limit was in the area and I still don't know today. We were caught by an officer with a handheld radar gun and the first I knew of it was when his colleague jumped out waving a small red lollipop sign. I pulled off the road onto the hard shoulder and the officer that was using the radar approached. It gradually dawned on him what he had stopped and his face lit up like a beacon. He called his fellow officer over eagerly whilst I pretended to be confused as to what was going on. He was talking excitedly to his colleague and pointing at the car so I said, "Beautiful?" in an enquiring fashion. "Yes, yes, beautiful," he replied. I reached behind me and withdrew a handful of postcards from the storage box and offered both the officers one each. It was then that I noticed the rear door of their patrol car open and an officer, with badges on his epaulettes signifying his seniority, stepped out. He started walking over to see what was going on so I quickly jumped out of the car and extended my hand to him. He took my hand and shook it, smiling as he moved closer to inspect the car. The junior officers made way for him and I held out a postcard towards him. He took it and looked at the picture of Bridget. I said, "For you," indicating with my hands that the card was a present. He spoke to the radar operator then turned to me and said, "Thank you. You go." I didn't need a second bidding.

We made our way without any undue events to Yazd. It appeared on the face of it to be just another provincial town but I was learning that in Iran external appearances can be deceptive. I was picked up by the tourist police at a road junction coming into town and given an escort to a hotel. From the outside it didn't look very promising but inside it was palatial.

Bridget was running so well that I considered continuing to Kerman, the next planned stop, but decided not to push too much before the 'robbers' road' in Pakistan. It would have been a total of over five hundred miles and the midday temperature was forty-seven degrees centigrade according to the television weather report. There's no doubt that leaving early in the morning and stopping around midday was much better for the car.

Saturday and we were another two hundred miles closer to Pakistan. We arrived at Kerman around midday and quickly found a Tourist Police car with three willing officers to escort us to a hotel. This time I was given a cold drink by the sergeant as well. On the drive we were flagged down a couple of times to have photos taken and were stopped twice at police checkpoints. A senior officer at the second checkpoint kindly gave me a bag of pistachio nuts, so all in all the 'boys in blue' were in favour for a while.

The standard of hotels throughout Iran is very good and the hotel at Kerman was no exception. I fell into the company of several students that used the hotel to 'chill out' and was invited out for the evening. I thought it was exceedingly nice of them to invite a 'wrinkly' along and it was a great opportunity to learn how they felt about the future of their country and their personal aspirations. They were surprisingly frank and confirmed a number of things that I had previously heard or that had been hinted at. The government is widely unpopular and their international policies have little support. The feeling seemed to be that if the UN was correct about nuclear weapons, the money could have been better spent on necessities for the people and that might also have removed the sanctions that were causing considerable inconvenience.

I also learnt that the religious police, that we heard so much about after the downfall of the Shah, are still very active, threatening peoples livelihoods and futures if they don't obey the strict codes of conduct, particularly things such as women's dress. One of the girl students told me that she liked to wear her headscarf in an individualistic manner whilst still making sure that it covered her head, as required by sharia law. She was stopped and admonished by the police who then reported her to the college where she studied and she was threatened with exclusion if she repeated the offence.

Sunday 3rd August and we arrived in Bam. The earthquake of four to five years earlier almost totally destroyed the city and the evidence of the devastation was still everywhere to be seen. Although building work was going on it appeared that more housing was desperately required.

The drive from Bam to Zahedan on the Iran/Pakistan border was a severe test for Bridget. The weather was extremely hot, plus there was a hot wind that felt similar to standing behind a jet plane's engine, and just to make it interesting there was a dust storm as well. The dust was very fine and got into everything. Visibility was reduced to under half a mile. It remained like that for almost the whole of the two hundred mile journey, which included traversing a mountain range. At least at the top of the mountains the dust was far less dense.

There was only one service station shown on the map and unfortunately when I arrived at the site it was all boarded up and deserted, so once again I had to use the jerry cans.

Anyway, we arrived safely and I took Bridget into a car wash to spruce her up. The guys that operate these washes just go mad over the car and do a very good job.

It was my intention to stay in Zahedan for two days' rest before tackling the robbers' road in Pakistan. The next day I checked the car over thoroughly in the hotel car park. The heat had taken a heavy toll in the cockpit, with much of the trim coming away as the glue melted. The crash bar foam had disintegrated into dust and the face of the speedometer had come adrift from the meter and flopped from side to side. In addition to this the oil filter was loose. Fluid levels were all OK except for the clutch reservoir, which I had expected to be dry from the difficulty I had finding second gear recently. Also, one of the front wheels had a little play in it so I removed that and found two things. The first was a nest of stowaways. Red ants had invaded the disc brake and they were swarming everywhere when I disturbed them by taking the wheel off. Secondly, the hub nut was indeed loose so I removed the split pin and tightened it up a notch. Whilst doing these minor adjustments a taxi driver arrived, amongst several other interested passers-by, and capably assisted, without being asked, as well as supplying a rag for cleaning up. Everything else appeared to be alright and ready to go.

As I checked out from the hotel in Zahedan the police arrived and insisted that I have an escort to the border for security reasons. They also had an Australian, Chris, with them who had driven a Toyota Landcruiser from the UK and was making for home taking the pretty route! We didn't clear Iranian customs until a little after midday. Entry into Pakistan was fairly swift but then we had to put our watches forward by one and a half hours so it was almost three in the afternoon by the time we were ready to go. The driver of the Ozbus was also at the Pakistan customs, having just driven from Quetta. The Ozbus plies between the UK and Australia on regular trips taking around three months each way. He told us that there was no way in this world the MG would get through the robbers road and added "You're bloody crazy, you'll wreck the car and have to walk out."

# INTO DANGER

*Location: Pakistan*
*Timeline: 6th August 2008 – 17th August 2008*

I was somewhat dispirited by what the Ozbus driver had said as he had just completed the drive that I was undertaking and broken his bus's suspension while doing so, but I was committed.

Returning outside from the Pakistan border post I spied an old Toyota pick-up truck with two camels lying down in the back of it. I quickly took out my camera and, making sure that only the truck with the camels was 'in picture', took a photograph. A cry went up and a Pakistani soldier ran over, clearly upset that I had taken a photograph. I knew that taking photos of the border post would not be allowed so quickly showed him the picture I had taken and the fact that it only showed the vehicle and camels. He impressed upon me that I should not take any photographs of the post, which was something of a joke as it only comprises of four ramshackle buildings.

It was clear that Chris's Toyota shouldn't have any problems with the terrain so we agreed to continue in our own time individually, but to try to keep in touch. I had read on some internet sites that the Pakistanis sometimes supplied escorts for security, but no escort was supplied and we were just told not to attempt to drive the road after dark as the lorries tend to drive straight down the middle and it's very dangerous. There is a small town called Dalbandin about halfway along the road so Chris and I thought we would try and make that before dark and then continue the next day.

Although I had fuelled up before leaving I was very aware of the distance we had to travel and that there might not be many filling stations en route. For a distance of around two kilometres from the border crossing there were hundreds, and possibly even thousands, of large plastic containers stacked up in blocks, varying from five to one hundred in each, all containing fuel. As I discovered, you just choose which pile looks best to you, pull over and tell the nearest man how much you want. They will then 'measure', and I use the term loosely, the required amount and pour it into your fuel tank. Unfortunately this type of casual storage ensures that you get more than just fuel pouring into your tank so I used my special funnel that has a filtering system to remove foreign bodies. It is not unusual for the 'attendant' to be smoking! Also, most of the fuel is illegally imported from Iran, although the retail cost is very nearly double.

Bridget and I arrived in Dalbandin at around six o'clock that evening and found a small hotel just inside the town boundary. A quick drive through the town confirmed that it was the only hotel, and anyway, the owner obviously had a sense of humour as a sign on the wall declared London Road Hotel. It was basic, if you get my drift, but it was only for one night and the cost was one pound twenty-five pence, including breakfast. On inspection of the room I found that the bed was clean so I accepted it after which the proprietor asked, "Would you like to sleep on the roof?" but I declined. A mistake; the night was very hot and, as I found out later, everyone outside the main cities sleep on the roofs. I decided to forgo breakfast and left early in the morning. Chris, the Australian, caught up with me a couple of hours into the journey; he had stayed in the police compound because they said the hotel in town wasn't safe!

The drive to Quetta was horrendous. There is a one hundred mile section where really there is no road. The best parts are surfaced but only a single vehicle wide with two way traffic and large potholes everywhere. Also, the desert is trying hard, and winning, to reclaim the road so there are a lot of sand drifts across the road/track. This lasts until a town called Nushki, after which there is another one hundred miles of mountain ranges. Here the road is better but still wouldn't be acceptable anywhere in Europe and the beautifully decorated lorries do tend to drive straight at you. As if this isn't enough, there are sleeping policemen (speed humps) at the entrance and exit of every town, before and after every railway line, at every school and every police checkpoint. There are, occasionally, some at locations where there used to be a checkpoint but they decided to remove it, leaving the speed hump. It was one of these that caught me full force at around forty-five miles per hour. Bridget took off but of course nosedived back to earth with a mighty crash. I pulled in to the side of the road to inspect the damage; fortunately nothing serious as far as I could see, but Bridget had lost a few bits and pieces. My stills camera which had been mounted on the windscreen had flown off across the road, the camera going one way and the mounting bracket another. I recovered both and amazingly the camera was still working.

We eventually arrived in full working order at the first 'safe city' of Quetta. The sump guard turned out to be a life saver. New springs and rear shock absorbers would have been a good idea too. But nothing beats a little British grit.

As we approached the city limits we were stopped at a police checkpoint. "Where are you from?" the officer asked. I told him the UK and presented my passport. "Where is your escort?" he asked. I replied that I didn't have an escort. "You have to have an escort," he then told me. I was becoming a little irritated now and said, "I am not going back for one if that's what you think." He looked sternly at me and commanded, "Wait." As he had my passport I decided that I would get out of the car and follow him into the post. He spoke to the senior officer there who then made a telephone call, I believe, to the border crossing. There was a heated discussion that was clearly about me and eventually he replaced the phone and spoke again to the first officer that I had seen. That officer then said to me, "You must have an escort at all times." With that I had to wait in my car until an escort in a Land Rover arrived and escorted me to a hotel. From then on I had an escort almost continuously, except when I could slip off unnoticed. In some locations I even had to have an escort to walk out of the hotel. This lasted until I arrived in Lahore.

Having been through a fairly tiring couple of days I decided that I would go to the other extreme and have a couple of days' luxury. I booked into the Quetta Serena Hotel, which, I have to say, is one of the best I have experienced anywhere. As you enter, through fairly extensive but necessary security, there is a calmness about the place. The service is world class and it was just what I needed. I also gave Bridget a six thousand mile service with the help of several members of the hotel staff, including some of their senior managers. They went all over town sourcing spare parts and even found a car wash where I could change the oil from within the water pit. It was during this operation that I discovered that one of her rear shock absorbers had broken. A spare could not be found so I had to execute a temporary repair using a two pound lump hammer and some chicken wire. Bridget was otherwise running really well again.

The plan was to leave Quetta early and take Route 65 to Sukkur. I had been told it was a good road and not at all like the robbers road.

I awoke at four thirty to the sound of explosions from incoming mortars and possibly some sort of rockets. They were landing quite close as the whole hotel vibrated and it was only a two storey building. I got dressed and went down to the lobby and out into the grounds. My instinct was that if we were under direct attack it would be safer outside than trapped inside. The security guards, who were all armed with either AK47s or pump action shot guns, were milling nervously around the extensive garden and car park area. The mortars stopped firing but were followed by the clatter of small arms fire. This continued for about an hour.

I went back in the lobby and spoke to the duty receptionist, asking if he could find out from the police if it would still be safe for me to travel that morning. He said he would phone them but after a short time informed me that, "They're not answering the phone because it's Sunday!" I suggested they weren't answering because someone was firing mortars at them and they were probably hiding under the table. Anyway, an hour later I decided to go ahead with my planned journey and so left the hotel and, travelling alone, found Route 65.

The first fifty miles were appalling, every bit as bad as the Taftan to Quetta road. Admittedly this was through a mountainous area but I thought that if this was considered a good road then I wanted out ASAP. There was an army convoy going in the same direction and as they were heavily armed I decided to join them for the security they offered. Eventually they turned off at a town called Mach and I continued alone. After a further twenty miles there was a police post and they were not happy about me travelling on my own so I was detailed an escort once more.

The escort system is operated by police in each separate district so you often have to wait at the district border, where invariably there is a checkpoint, until your next escort comes to meet you.

The following one hundred miles of road were really very acceptable but for the last one hundred miles it deteriorated again, with deep potholes and a generally bumpy surface. I was conscious the whole time of the broken shock absorber and just hoping that the temporary repair would hold. The journey took ten hours with no comfort break, because the police have other duties, and my stomach chose this morning to have its first upset (nothing to do with the mortars, more to do with a Chinese dinner!).

On arriving at Sukkur I had a shower, a rest and drank lots of water, then I decided to take a short walk to get the lie of the land. I had not gone more the twenty paces out of the grounds and the security guard came running up to me and told me that it was unsafe for me to walk out without an armed escort. I was therefore a virtual prisoner with no facilities in the hotel.

It is a source of regret that I cannot say that Pakistan, like Iran, is a beautiful country with a largely warm, friendly population. The region of Balochistan has beautiful mountains and, though not to everyone's taste, wonderful desert areas. Some of the people are very friendly and hospitable, but unfortunately many treated me with suspicion and a lack of respect. Certainly the region is extremely poor; the towns dirty, smelly and exceptionally basic. It was absolutely clear that the people and local officials believe that they are discriminated against by the Central Government in Lahore, which may be true, but the lifestyle certainly creates a potential recruiting ground for extreme elements.

I left Sukkur at six thirty in the morning, along with my police escort, the temporary repair to the shock absorber still intact. After about twenty miles heading north the scenery changed quite rapidly, with much more greenery about. They grow rice, sugar, cotton and cereals here. The further towards Lahore we went the cleaner the towns were and the more prosperous people appeared, although still poor by Western standards.

My police escort had been absolutely brilliant, with smooth efficient changeovers such that I really only stopped the once for refuelling in the whole two hundred and eighty miles. One of the escort vehicles did throw up a stone and cracked Bridget's windscreen, so that was another thing to add to my list of repairs needed. I decided I would spend a few days in Lahore sorting things out for Bridget.

What a challenge. I was told that I was mad (again) to visit Pakistan and at times I wondered if the best option was to get to the nearest airport and go home to my loved ones.

I found Pakistan to be a country divided by religion, but with common desires amongst all of the different groups. Their most ardent wish was for peace and an end to lawlessness and corruption. The image presented to us in Europe and the USA, of a militant religious population led by groups of terrorists and supporters, was very far from the truth. By and large the radical militants were a very small minority and they were shunned by most of the population. Much of the violence in the country was directed not at Western interests, but at Pakistani interests and people, and the general population was upset that we should believe the worse of them.

I found the southern areas that I visited extremely poor but the Punjab was far more prosperous. Agriculture in the Punjab was good, the country was green, even lush in some areas, and the towns were much cleaner with good employment prospects. That was not to say everything was rosy, the country's economy was a disaster and their politicians were lightweight and unable to cope.

Lahore, like many other ex-colonial cities, retained the best things from the days of the British Empire. There was evidence of this all over the city: street signs, buildings, city archives, the railways and even in some of the peoples' customs such as 'high tea'. The people of all persuasions were fiercely patriotic, as witnessed at the Wagah border crossing ceremony held every evening and the Independence Day celebrations.

The 14th August is Independence Day in Pakistan and there are enthusiastic celebrations throughout the country. Bridget and I arrived in Lahore on the morning of this momentous day, totally unaware of the revelry that was to take place later. Having booked into a hotel I decided to explore the local area during the afternoon. As I was leaving one of the concierge said, "Do not to stay out too long," because the evening would get fairly boisterous. I smiled and politely thanked him for his advice without understanding what he meant.

By mid afternoon it was obvious from the banners that appeared everywhere that today was Independence Day. There were also people everywhere wearing all sorts of garments coloured green and white and sporting badges of the national flag. As the afternoon wore on vehicles drove aimlessly about, with passengers carrying all sizes of flags and waving them from the windows or out of sunshine roofs. As dusk fell large numbers of people, many in family groups, took to the streets and parks singing, shouting and being generally rowdy in support of their country. I was stopped by many groups asking where I was from and urging me to join in, which I was happy to do for a time before passing on to another group somewhere down the road.

The most extreme celebrations, however, took place on the roads. In addition to the flag carrying cars there were thousands of small engine motorbikes, in the main 125ccs. Anywhere from an individual to a small family would travel on these with up to seven abreast across a single carriageway. Many of the youths did wheelies and other antics through the traffic that is so dense that crossing the road was almost impossible. Although the police initially tried to stop the excesses, and television news programmes reminded people of the dangers of these activities, they were performed throughout the night. The following day the media constantly updated the death and injury figures caused by road accidents the previous evening.

Two days later I attended the Wagah border flag lowering ceremony. The Wagah border crossing was the only site where vehicles could legally cross from Pakistan into India and vice versa. Every day the individual countries raise and lower their respective flags at the gates marking the crossing point, with the evening ceremony having been developed into a popular tourist attraction. The highly trained border troops from both countries go through a well rehearsed ceremonial ritual of closing the gates then lowering their flags with lots of mock aggression and good natured taunting. The whole show takes around an hour and is very worthy of a visit.

There was one amusing and totally un-rehearsed event during the ceremony. Before the official procedures began there were a number of individuals dressed in their national colours who went through rituals, whipping up vocal support from the crowd. They carried huge national flags and shouted slogans, to which the crowd replied. It had started quietening down when a voice from the crowd yelled out one of the slogans, starting it all up again. I turned to see who had shouted out and it was a Japanese tourist! Anyway, turning back to the action I noticed that one of the Pakistani army sergeants had approached one of the crowd agitators, an elderly gentleman that must have been in his seventies. They stood side by side and the sergeant said something out of the corner of his mouth whilst trying to look nonchalant. It reminded me of the old trick of saying to someone in the public eye, "Do you know your fly is undone?" Anyway, the gentleman looked up at his flag with a look of horror on his face. The two of them commenced a hurried and clearly serious discussion whilst looking at the flag, and then the old gentleman lowered the pole and the sergeant removed the flag. Then ensued further debate and the flag was turned this way and that and eventually was replaced, to the old man's obvious relief. Clearly there must be a right and a wrong way up for the Pakistani flag, just as there is with the Union Jack, and the sergeant had noticed that this one was wrong, but it made for an amusing interlude, all of which I captured on video.

The following day Bridget and I would pass through this crossing into another of our destinations en route.

All in all I was sorry to leave Pakistan; I had met some beautiful people there, but India was calling and so was my need to travel.

# COUNTRY OF THE OLD RAJ

*Location: India*
*Timeline: 18th August 2008 – 11th September 2008*

The difference is immediately noticeable as you drive down the road over the Wagah border crossing from Pakistan into India. Everything is cleaner, the population more prosperous and even the traffic is more 'up-market'. The atmosphere is also more relaxed as people do not have to worry about whether or not they will be returning home in the evening.

None of that is to decry Pakistan and I stand by everything I have already said, but there is a difference and it is very noticeable.

We went straight to Amritsar, a journey of around thirty five miles. Amritsar is an unremarkable city with one or two places to visit plus a trump card in any game: the Golden Temple. I had heard of it from news bulletins and I knew it was the central place of worship for the Sikhs. I had even seen television pictures of it, but nothing prepares you for the spectacle that is the temple itself. Nothing I can write will do it justice; all I can say is if you ever get the opportunity to visit it, grasp it with both hands.

At each entrance there are large facilities for you to remove and safely store your shoes, as no footware is allowed in the temple. Entering through archways you move from shaded areas into brilliant sunshine, made all the more fierce by the beautiful white marble that makes up most of the temple. There are large bright blue pools which you may bathe in if you wish and in the centre is the temple itself, a gleaming gold structure, distinct against the white marble. Everyone is made to feel welcome and offered various tasty local dishes to eat. The whole place is exceptionally clean and obviously loved and cared for. It's a fascinating place just to walk around and watch the people.

Throughout Pakistan I had been having trouble getting ATMs to work and I even called the bank back in the UK in case they had blocked my card. They told me they thought it was either a problem with the machines or a network problem within Pakistan. Now in Amritsar and very short of cash, I tried some more ATMs. The problem persisted and so I called the UK again and related the problem. The operator made some checks and transferred the call to their security department. Once they had security checked me the operator said, "Oh, yes we have blocked the card. Someone was trying to use it in Pakistan, you know!"

Bridget's engine still had a tendency to backfire when she was first started but settled down after a short run. I would really have liked to check the timing and I knew that one of the carburettors had an air leak. I would have to overhaul the carburettors in Australia as well as refurbishing the shock absorbers and possibly replacing the rear springs.

From Amritsar we drove down to Ambala, which is on the main route to Delhi, however that was not my objective on this occasion. I had arranged with a chap at the hotel in Amritsar to leave Bridget at a hotel in Ambala and then be driven up to Mcleodganj in the Himachal Pradesh region. The idea was to go trekking in the mountains there, an area of outstanding beauty.

Just as well I left Bridget behind this time as the road we took was still waiting to be built. There was also some tree felling going on supposedly beside the road. Just moments after I was wondering, "What would happen if they got it wrong?" we ground to a halt in a long line of traffic. Sure enough the road was blocked by …a fallen tree! After about an hour they managed to make a large enough gap for single line traffic to pass.

At Mcleodganj, sometimes called Little Lhasa, is the residence of the Dalai Lama and the exiled Government of Tibet. Close by I also viewed St John's Church, which could have been a church in any English village except for the corrugated iron roof over the tower.

From there I went to Dharamkot with a beautiful panoramic view of the Kangra Valley, Pong Dam and Dhauladhar mountain range. I went mountain trekking on the Saturday for just over 11 kilometres, climbing to a height of two thousand eight hundred metres, and it was just beautiful. The wildlife was interesting with monkeys galore and several mongooses, or should that be mongeese, including one on the balcony of my hotel room.

From there it was back to Ambala to collect Bridget and then, after a good nights sleep, on to Delhi. On arriving back at the hotel, just as I thought this was the end of this part of my journey, there was an Indian wedding taking place. I asked the hotel manager if it would be alright to take one or two photos and he said it would be no problem.

Whilst taking the first photo I was spotted by the groom's mother who immediately insisted that I join them. I held back, not wishing to intrude on the couples' day, but I was gradually coaxed into the proceedings and ended up having my photo taken with the happy couple.

New Delhi is a clean modern city that contains the embassies, tourist hotels and shopping centres that most modern capital cities have. However, there is also old Delhi, which is a little run down and doesn't really give a damn about tourists preferring to stay the way it's always been. Nothing wrong with that, but it also wants to attract the financial benefits brought by tourists without putting in the effort of making them feel welcome. Of course they can't have it both ways and the epitome of this dilemma is the Red Fort.

This site is in desperate need of cleaning, a little maintenance and some entrepreneurial flair. When you consider the basic offering, it is tired, dirty and in need of some renovation (a little like me really). It is registered as a world heritage site, but is poorly cared for. However, with cleaning, a little restoration and some imagination it could be a major international attraction. If the site was improved, even superficially, and a group of people acting as soldiers were introduced, dressed in the uniforms from the days of the British Raj, with two flag raising or lowering ceremonies each day, a little like the Wagah border, this would be a fantastic attraction.

There is also the Jantar Mantar observatory, an interesting attraction built in the eighteenth century employing large brick built astronomy instruments, and there are several other sites of interest, such as the India Gate, but I was underwhelmed at the offerings of such a culturally rich capital city.

To cap it all I caught a cold, or I hoped that's what it was as there was a near epidemic of dengue fever in Delhi. The papers were claiming that the health service hospitals had no vacant beds, little medicine and that patients were being discharged before they were well. A bit like the UK but without the problem of MRSA!

I decided we would move on to Agra and the Taj Mahal.

Agra is, I'm told, a city of some two and a half million inhabitants, but there is little to recommend it to tourists other than the obvious Taj Mahal.

Visiting some of these world famous sites that we have all read about, or seen on television, does not always live up to our expectations and I have to say that the Taj is one of them as far as I was concerned. I far preferred the Golden Temple in Amritsar where my expectations, due to my ignorance, were low, but that said the site was far cleaner and better presented than the Taj Mahal. A little like the Red Fort in Delhi, the Taj needs cleaning and the grounds require far better maintenance.

Most major tourist authorities around the world, in charge of sites that I have had the privilege of seeing, make an effort to present not only the site to the best of its ability, but also the surrounding area. The conditions in Agra, I am afraid to say, are that the roads are atrocious, the streets strewn with rubbish and goodness knows what else, and there are really none of the facilities that you would expect in the immediate vicinity of the site, such as quality souvenir or book stores. It appears that the official attitude is "this site attracts thousands every year without our having to make any worthwhile investment."

Beware if you do visit the Taj and hope to leave with a videoed memory of the site. On entry through the outer gate you have to pay to take your camera with you, but that only allows you to video the area up to the main gate. You will not be allowed to take it inside the main gate. Although the filming of the interior grounds is forbidden, I somehow came into the possession of some footage, but if you are caught filming you may be ejected.

I have said little or nothing, to date, about the animal life that abounds in Pakistan and India, partly because I have little or no knowledge of the names of many species. However, those interested in butterflies would have a field day, particularly in the mountains of the Himachal Pradesh region. The only one that I recognised was a "pintail", I believe it's called. The colours of some are simply dazzling and some are the size of your hand. I noticed that some species appear to live in colonies and form a small cloud around their habitat.

I did mention, in my introduction to India, the mongoose, which I have found to be very common and fascinating to watch. Their young are very playful and appear to have quite a personality. Otherwise there are camels, water buffalo and on the drive from Delhi to Agra I rounded a corner to be faced by an elephant. It had a handler with it, thank goodness, and its head was brightly decorated (the elephant's not the handler's) which I believe is quite common.

Animals are a considerable road hazard, with carts being pulled by horses, donkeys and asses; I have even seen a moke, camels, buffalo and Indian domestic cows. It is not at all unusual to find a group of cows, not enough to call them a herd, sleeping in the middle of a highway and there are lots of wild dogs that run out without warning.

Finally, the bird population is fascinating with every colour imaginable. I have seen Hoopoe, a Maharatta woodpecker with a magnificent red crescent, and a Rosy-ringed parakeet.

The drive from Agra to Jaipur was easy and uneventful, taking three and a half hours to cover one hundred and eighty miles. However, I then spent another two hours driving around the city trying to find the Holiday Inn, receiving numerous conflicting directions from Jaipur's traffic police. Then to cap it all, a boy on an overloaded bicycle misjudged the amount of space he needed and ripped off my nearside mirror whilst I was waiting at some traffic lights. On the basis that the cost of a replacement would be more than six months wages for him, I put it down to experience and added it to the list of parts required when I arrived in Perth. I hoped the MG club would be well stocked with spares!

Jaipur is also known as the Pink City, so called because of the colour of the local building material. Compared to other cities that I have visited in India it appears more compact, but not more overcrowded than usual, cleaner, and, although they have many more tourist attractions than most, they are investing in restoring and improving the sites.

I stayed for two nights at the Rambagh Palace which until very recent times was the home to the Maharaja of Jaipur. Jaipur is the capital of Rajasthan, home to the Rajputs a group of warrior clans who ruled this part of India for over a thousand years. The palace has been turned into a hotel to ensure it remains in excellent condition and the late Maharaja's cars are available for guests to hire. A beautifully restored 1958 Dodge asked to have its photo taken with Bridget, a request that I duly fulfilled.

I was starting to give serious thought to the task of getting to Australia and currently the plan was to go down to Goa for a short piece of R&R and then over to Chennai in about three weeks. On that basis we would arrive in Perth in around six to seven weeks' time.

Whilst in Jaipur I had a stinking cold for several days and my legs broke out in heat bumps caused by the temperature in the cars footwell. When I awoke the next day I went to get out of bed and collapsed on the floor in agony. I had no idea what was wrong but the top of my left thigh felt as if it had been hit with a baseball bat. I could only just walk and kept making involuntary gasps of pain. A real wimp. Anyway, I managed to lever myself into the car and left at eight o'clock on Sunday 31st August for Udaipur. The journey was just under three hundred miles and I only stopped the once for fuel.

Sometimes things happen that could not be written in a fiction novel because they seem so bizarre. I actually checked Udaipur hotels on the internet, which I almost never do, and selected one that sounded better than the others in the affordable range. Having been given varying instructions on how to find the hotel, by traffic police again, all different, I hired a motor rickshaw and followed him. I would not have found the place in a hundred years and the track up to it, together with the initial view as we approached, made me a little apprehensive. It looked a little scruffy and run down at first glance but as we got closer I noticed an excellent cricket pitch. My first thought was that this had to be separate from the hotel, but it was not.

With the usual interest being expressed over the car at reception, I checked in. After resting in my room for half an hour I walked outside to explore, because although the track to the hotel appeared dirty and dusty, as well as the cricket pitch I had spied polo ponies in paddocks, a stable block and a small aerodrome! It transpired that this was the hunting lodge belonging to the Maharana of Udaipur and he had had it turned into a country hotel. I was reliably informed that a Maharana is senior to a Maharaja in the old order of things.

Early in the evening I was apprehended walking across the front courtyard and asked to go with the gentleman to reception. "Ah Mr Locock," said the receptionist, "it so happens that the Maharana has an MG Midget (an MG TC as it turned out) amongst his collection of twenty-eight or so vintage vehicles and his chief mechanic has taken the liberty of looking yours over." He continued, "He heard you arrive earlier and says that you have a carburettor problem and we would like to offer his services together with our garage to assist you by repairing it if we have the parts."

I was speechless, though only for a moment, and stood up rapidly from my seat forgetting all about my leg problem, and almost falling over gave out a yelp.

So I was to meet the head mechanic the next morning and we would discuss an action plan. It may have meant staying an extra couple of days, but that would give my leg a rest. I had also been invited to view the Maharana's collection, and what a collection it is. It includes the 1934 Rolls Royce Phantom II used in the James Bond film *Octopussy*, a 1938 Cadillac convertible used on a state visit by Her Majesty the Queen, a customised Rolls Royce Jeep and a 1946 MG TF.

Shriji Arvind Singh Mewar, Maharana of Udaipur, is an avid collector of cars and also a proud member of the MG Owners Club of the UK. His collection is held in the Vintage and Classic Car Collection that is, in fact, an annex of the Garden Hotel, which he also owns and was once his main palace residence.

Given the fantastic motors that his mechanics have in their charge, I had every confidence in their ability to work on Bridget and it wasn't misplaced. By the time the chief mechanic stopped for lunch the transmission and gearbox oil had been checked and topped up, the rear brake shoes adjusted, the air filters removed and cleaned, and the twin carburettors stripped, cleaned and re-assembled. The timing was then checked and the car returned to me sounding almost perfect. They were unable to completely fix things as some replacement parts were needed that they would have to order from the UK and I didn't want to stay around for another week waiting.

From Udaipur the plan was to drive to Vadodara to stay over night, but I couldn't find the hotel. This was the second time I had tried to stay at a Holiday Inn but had been totally unable to locate it. Either my navigation is rubbish, or their directions leave something to be desired. Given that I had found my way over eight thousand miles successfully, I think my navigation was reasonably average.

As there was still plenty of time I decided we should strike out for Pune, which was to have been the next stop after Vadodara, some two hundred and fifty miles further on. Unfortunately the road surface deteriorated again making progress painfully slow and it soon became obvious that to reach my destination that day I would have to drive in the dark, something I had avoided doing previously. Then to make things a little more interesting the heavens opened and it poured with rain. When it does this in India it really is extreme. As I found out a couple of days later, Pune received seventy-four millimetres of rain in twenty-four hours, leaving much of the town under some two feet of water.

By five o'clock in the afternoon the storm made it so dark that it was just like driving at night. This was when I discovered that eighty-five out of every one hundred Indian HGVs don't have rear lights. Most are broken but some are just painted over! I had noticed before, to my amusement, that many trucks have hand painted bodywork and often the 'artist' had found it easier and quicker when doing the rear to just paint over everything: doors (if they were still there), hinges, number plates and lights.

After struggling for a couple of hours through this nightmare I decided that if I continued I would wreck the car because it was impossible to see the pot holes in time to avoid them, so I started searching for a hotel. I found a suitable looking establishment in a town called Vapi and stayed the night. All things considered it was the right thing to do.

The following day I found Pune and a totally different piece of India. Within the city limits they have built a complete Italian style village. There are several large modern industrial complexes, either built or nearing completion, that are identical to the modern complexes all over Western Europe. This is the software capital of India. Most of the big names are based here and that means there is a large influx of foreign investment, which shows in the lifestyle of the local population.

Still, I wanted to press on to the state of Goa and some R&R. I was still nursing a very heavy cold, heat bumps on my legs and a generally run down feeling. I was sure that it was the constant stress of scanning the road for danger, in addition to all the other things driving in this part of the world demands, which had tired me.

The drive from Pune to Candolim in Goa started far better than I could have expected. We joined National Highway Four just outside Pune and headed south, following the signs for Bengaluru. The condition of the road was good for most of the two hundred miles to Belgaum, where we turned off towards Panaji. I guess after that I shouldn't complain, but most of the next one hundred miles was absolutely diabolical. The exception was one short stretch of road, of around five miles, over a mountain range. The surface was not perfect but the road is one of those that MGs were built for, climbing fairly steeply and snaking around often completely blind corners. Traffic in India is not fazed by blind corners or the brows of hills and completely ignores them when overtaking, so it is not unusual to find two vehicles heading in opposite directions at a standstill, nose to nose.

As we neared Panaji, the state capital, we hit another unmarked 'speed breaker', as they misguidedly call them; 'suspension breaker' is a far more accurate description, and they were totally unnecessary as the general condition of the road surface prohibits speed of more than fifteen miles per hour anyway. Fortunately, this time there was no permanent damage but another wheel cap had disappeared.

We arrived at the hotel in Candolim at around four o'clock. Goa was once the capital of Portugal's eastern empire and evidence of its influence is all about, particularly in many of the buildings. It gives it a sort of Bahamas flavour. The people here are warm, friendly and genuinely hospitable, being only too happy to assist in any way they can.

Three days R&R is what was ordered and that was what we were going to have, after which it would be onto Chennai and pack-up for Australia.

The time spent in Candolim was just what I needed. I met up with a lovely English couple (well almost English, from Watford) who were kind enough to take the old man under their wing. We had a great time and I thank them.

The day before we were scheduled to leave Candolim I noticed that the rear near-side tyre was a little deflated. I found a garage with an airline just down from the hotel and they agreed to inflate it for me. However, the tyre didn't want to play and on closer inspection I found it was badly cut in several places. This was obviously as a result of the road conditions coming into Goa. The guys at the garage quickly replaced the wheel with the spare but we weren't able to get a replacement tyre so I just had to hope that we wouldn't get another puncture.

There are two alternative main routes from Candolim to Bangalore, the overnight stopping point en route to Chennai. The first would be to retrace our steps to the main highway NH4, but I knew that the first one hundred mile stretch would be awful. The second route runs down the Goan coast on highway NH17 to Mangalore and then on NH48 to Bangalore. This route was strongly recommended and so that was the direction we set out on.

Major mistake; although the route is quite beautiful in places, the chance to see and appreciate it is rare as you struggle across large tracts of rocky washed out roads. The tracts can be anything up to two miles long. Our average speed was twenty miles per hour and it took ten and a half hours to reach Mangalore, a distance of two hundred and fifty-five miles. I decided we could not continue further that day and found a hotel for the night.

On checking into a reasonable looking hotel in the centre of the city, the receptionist quietly suggested that I might like to park Bridget in a private garage at the rear of the hotel. At first I thought that this was so potential thieves would not see it, but it transpired that we had arrived during an outbreak of religious riots between Hindus and Christians. As a European I would be assumed to be Christian and therefore a potential target. After I had moved Bridget I was shown to my room by the usual bellhop, who stopped and, looking around rather apprehensively to ensure nobody could overhear us, he whispered, "I'm a Christian." With this he smiled and shot off down the corridor. I found it terribly sad that anyone felt so threatened for holding a religious belief and sharing that knowledge with someone else. Unfortunately I have a fairly black sense of humour at times and as he scuttled down the corridor it occurred to me that I should have whispered back "...and I'm a Hindu," but fortunately I held my peace.

Mangalore to Bangalore is two hundred and twenty miles and it took us some eight and a half hours to cover, an improvement over the previous day but most of the time was spent on the first one hundred miles. Again much of the road was no more than a very bad track. I was amazed that Bridget was still in one piece as the conditions were as extreme as any found in Pakistan.

Just to make the journey appealing, fate had one more surprise for us. The route after the first hundred miles is a single carriageway of reasonable condition, although you still have to be on the lookout for large potholes. These can be very difficult, particularly if they occur whilst you are overtaking, as there is little room to avoid them. The procedure for overtaking is to sit on the tail of the vehicle in front, sound your horn several times to ensure they know you are there and then execute the manoeuvre. This is done whether or not on a blind bend, approaching the brow of a hill or just on a clear stretch of road, ignoring, of course, cyclists, pedestrians, water buffalo, stray dogs, etc.

HGVs are always a problem and on this type of route are almost always in short convoys. It was one of these convoys, of gas tankers, that caused me to consider the new sport of 'jungle driving'. I had carried out the routine horn blowing and started to overtake the first of the tankers (or last, depending on your perspective) in the line when it decided to cut the corner of a slight right-hand curve in the road. Of course, as we were alongside it meant that the room available to us was narrowing from six feet to just one. The choice was simple, have the side of Bridget ripped off or take a diversion into the jungle on the offside of the road. Unfortunately the way the road is constructed means that along much of it there is a 'shoulder' that is around a foot deep. That's about nine inches too much for the car and so there was a terrible grating noise, a great deal of bumping and a portion of screeching (I think the last bit may have been me). Somehow we avoided the larger parts of the vegetation and actually made it back onto the road ahead of the tanker! The driver, or aimer is probably a more accurate description in India, realised what had happened, braked and pulled over to the nearside to give us, rather belatedly, some room.

Bridget's engine was still running and the gauges still registering as normal. All four wheels were still attached as was almost everything else except the rear number plate, which was hanging down on one side. I used a wiring strap to fix the plate and drove on. On cursory examination the area around the differential was badly scraped and the brake piping had been bent but that appeared to be the only damage. We continued on without further event to Bangalore.

Just as I was about to leave the hotel the next day, there was the usual huddle of interested people around Bridget when the crowd parted to let a fellow Englishman through. John, an engineer with BA, had been in India for three months. Although our conversation was necessarily short it was good to touch base with someone from home, even though only momentarily.

The following day we continued to Chennai, with little excitement, and Bridget was to be thoroughly cleaned before being handed over to the shipping agent. I had been told to have her steam cleaned otherwise Australian quarantine would not allow us in. As it transpired, there are no facilities in Chennai for steam cleaning and I couldn't even get a competent wash for her. I would just have to hope to resolve the matter in Oz.

I located the shipping agent who was to complete the paperwork, and pack and clear Bridget through customs and I had to accompany him to the customs office. This visit took a whole day, at the end of which I was told we would have to return the next day as the senior official had gone home. We duly presented ourselves again at nine-thirty the next morning and were accompanied to the container packing site by the senior customs official. Once he had cleared the car, all that remained was for Bridget to be driven into her container. This was the first time I had gone through this procedure and so wasn't sure what to expect. I had noticed a small elderly gentleman arrive a little earlier on an ancient Rayleigh bicycle with lengths of 2x1 timber strapped to the crossbar. Once Bridget was incarcerated in her container this gentleman advanced with a tape measure and after taking several measurements removed the timber from his bicycle and made a wooden frame. This was then fitted around Bridget to prevent her from moving whilst being transported to the ship, loaded or during her voyage.

The first leg of the challenge had taken us through eleven different countries, covering over eleven thousand miles. There were certainly times when I thought we wouldn't get to this point, but there was never an instant when I regretted trying.

There were a great number of experiences that I will never forget and some that I would rather, but my lasting memory will always be the people that I met along the way; the warmth, friendliness and general helpfulness that they so freely offered. It really started in Vienna and grew with every new country I visited, but perhaps in Iran more than anywhere.

The tourist sight that made the most impression was, by far, the Golden Temple; simply amazing. Then there were the termite houses in Kandovan, the Wagah border ceremony and the Jantar Mantar observatory in Delhi.

The most memorable natural spectacles were the picturesque mountains along the Caspian coast in Astara, the wilderness area of the Pakistan/Afghanistan border, and the mountains of Himachel Pradesh.

Bridget had been, in so many ways, the hero of the adventure to date. The punishment that the car had borne would have caused many much younger, more robust and suitably designed vehicles to give up the ghost. The list of parts required had gradually grown and included new shock absorbers, rear springs, a passenger side wing mirror, a windscreen, hub covers and headlamp protectors. It was quite likely that there would be more once we got it onto a hoist and examined it properly, particularly the steering.

But at the end of this first leg the single most memorable happening was an encounter I had with a family in a park in Pakistan. It is a regular thing for families to all go to the parks in the evenings just to enjoy family time together and take in their surroundings. This particular family included nine children, five dressed in matching clothes, whose ages ranged from the baby to around eleven years. They had spied this 'foreigner' and one of them summoned up the courage to run over and say "Hello" and then hastily run away. The others, not to be outdone, quickly joined in until all of them, one carrying their baby brother, came to 'talk' to the stranger. Eventually their parents, who spoke good English, came and joined us and for a while it reminded me that I had two lovely grand daughters who I hadn't seen for some months.

# BOTTOM OF THE WORLD

*Location: Australia*
*Timeline: 30th September 2008 to 27th February 2009*

Whilst Bridget was at sea, en route to Australia, I decided to take a couple of weeks' rest in Phuket, Thailand. I truly hadn't realised how tired I was and this break turned out to be just what was needed to re-invigorate myself.

Fremantle is Western Australia's principle port, and more or less a suburb of Perth, the largest city in Western Australia. Originally established as a port for the Swan Valley Colony, this is where many migrants in the 19th and early 20th centuries first set foot on Australian soil and this is where Bridget the Midget would come ashore from Chennai in India. I posed as a tourist until she was due and discovered that many of the architectural features of Fremantle are the original port wharves extensively restored and converted into retail and residential buildings. A considerable number are now owned and occupied by Fremantle's Notre Dame University, including the old Customs House, P & O Hotel, and the Orient Hotel.

Fremantle Prison, due to become a World Heritage site in 2009, gives an interesting insight into one side of life in the early years of colonisation, although the forty criminals executed there may not agree. Additionally, Fremantle has many museums, art galleries, including aboriginal art and art from past inmates of the prison, and general tourist sites.

Perth, the capital city of Western Australia, is 20 kilometres north of Fremantle. A cosmopolitan city, the architecture is a peculiar mixture of the extremely modern and 19th century British. The restored town hall was modelled on an English Jacobean market hall, His Majesty's Theatre has an opulent Georgian exterior and St George's Cathedral would look at home in any old English town or village. However, the links with the UK are not all old, as the Swan Bell Tower is testament to. Housed in a contemporary structure in Perth's Barrack Square, the collection of bells include the Twelve Bells of St Martin-in-the-Fields, the church in Trafalgar Square in London. These were gifted to Perth to mark the bicentenary in 1988.

I noticed that the Australians appear to be able to turn almost anything into a tourist attraction: bells, boats, prisons and old warehouses. Being 'caught short' one afternoon I felt I had to make sure that the public toilet wasn't on the tour schedule before going in.

There is also a very strong coffee house and restaurant culture. With 95% of the population resident around the coastal belt of the country, it is not surprising to find that seafood is very prominent in the diet and amongst the best in the world.

I arrived in Fremantle a week before Bridget was due and acquainted myself with the city and the local MG Car Club. I had been met at the airport by three members of the club's committee and David Pitcher, the editor of the club magazine, showed me around Perth and Fremantle.

The first place he took me was Kings Park, which looks right across Perth and gives you a good idea of its layout. Purely coincidently, there was a gathering of the British Riley Car Club assembling in the car park as we arrived, which acted as an indication of the number of classic cars in Australia. Three days later was a Sunday and as I walked out of my hotel in Fremantle I could see cars gathering on the green across the road. It turned out to be a meeting of the Austin Car Club and later in the morning, on the same green, a meeting was held by the French Car Clubs representing Citroen, Renault and Peugeot. I read somewhere that there are forty two car clubs in Western Australia alone.

The weekend that Bridget was due to arrive, however, I spent many hours at the dockside in Fremantle watching ships come and go.

Almost unbelievably I had been given the wrong name of the container ship bringing Bridget to Perth and it had in fact docked during the Saturday. I found this out the following Monday and the immigration inspection was arranged for Wednesday, along with the customs clearance. Customs duly gave her the OK and signed the carnet form but to her dismay she was judged by the quarantine inspector to be *too dirty* to be allowed entry! The shame; she was mortified.

I had been cautioned that this was likely as almost every car privately imported has to go through a thorough cleaning to remove any engine fluids, dirt, vegetation and, most importantly, any insects that may have hitched a ride from another country. This action is to protect the Australian habitat, indigenous wildlife and farming. The interior of the car, as well as the exterior and the boot, has to be cleaned and examined. What amazed me, however, is that the cleaning took four days, after which it was re-examined and, once approved, it was allowed into the country.

When that stage was complete I had to get a visitor's permit to drive her to a vehicle roadworthiness inspection centre, which is similar to the UK's MOT check. I was allowed to take it first to The Sports Garage in Perth where they kindly made some workshop space available together with tools, equipment and even the assistance of some expert hands. After the work was completed and the roadworthiness inspection had been done, we were ready to start our passage across the south coast to Adelaide and Melbourne. The new schedule would start around the end of the month.

The planned route from Perth would be south to Albany and on to Esperance, an area, I was told, of outstanding beauty. From there would be my first 'long drive' to Adelaide, then on to Geelong and Melbourne. Many people warned me that some of the driving I would be undertaking around Australia was going to be monotonous.

The dangers on the roads in Australia, there are always some unique to every country, are basically kangaroos and roadtrains. Kangaroos, because of the way they leap, have a tendency to appear from nowhere and, as some can be over six feet tall, it would only require one to wreck the car should we hit it at speed. The second danger, roadtrains, are even bigger; up to fifty-three metres in length and weighing up to two hundred and fifty tonnes. Not unlike the forty tonne HGVs in the UK at the front, they tow up to four trailers! Firstly, passing these safely requires long stretches of clear road, which is plentiful in the sparsely inhabited Northern Territories, and secondly, once rolling these vehicles aren't slow, being legally allowed to travel at up to one hundred and ten kilometres an hour. On the plus side, however, unlike in Asia, they do have working lights and indicators, they are not brightly painted with messages of Christian love and they do not generally drive down the middle of the road.

Regarding the condition of the roads, most of those I planned to use were, I was informed, tarmac covered and smooth. There might possibly be some that were not metalled in the interior and the northern state, but they should be fine as long as it didn't rain! Summer was however the wet season in the north so it could prove interesting.

The week before starting there was plenty of activity, starting with an MG Car Club event. It was a two day drive, well supported with sixty-four entries, and I was honoured to be asked to 'wave it off'. I had been working each day on returning Bridget to full health, under the excellent guidance of Tim Harland, and a lot of things had needed doing. It was interesting from my perspective as it felt almost as if, for the first time in forty years, I had returned to a normal eight to five job without any management problems or worries. I even felt guilty one morning when I was late arriving, caused by calling into a bank.

To round off my stay in Perth, I watched the Red Bull Air Race, a change from cars. Although not my particular preference as a pastime, it was thrilling and the pilots are extremely skilful.

After a short farewell from a number of the members of the MG Car Club, Bridget and I left Perth set for Albany on our first drive in Australia. The trip lasted around four hours and was uneventful. I stopped off for coffee at the Wool Sheds in Williams, a small town some ninety miles south of Perth. The Wool Sheds are a typical local product/craft centre for tourists. This particular one specialises in clothes made from local wool. The Marino items were fantastic, so soft.

I'm not sure if it was something I said, but I must have upset someone in Perth for them to send me to Albany. They said it is beautiful and would remind me of England, and I guess it did in a way, as it rained all day and the wind off the sea was bitterly cold.

The architecture put me in mind of the frontier towns of the early colonial days, some being little more than wooden sheds and some grand with beautiful verandas and balconies. I really rather liked it. Many of the buildings, of course, are from that era and those built later have been sympathetic to them. There is the first consecrated Anglican church of Australia, erected in 1848, and a town hall, built in 1886, that would look perfectly at home in many Northern or Midland towns in England.

My first fleeting view of Princess Royal Harbour immediately put me in mind of the television pictures of Goose Green in the Falklands, with hills down to the water's edge and the water being whipped by strong winds, under very overcast skies.

The countryside en route was largely bush with some cereal farming and rolling hills similar, to those in the UK.

Day two in Albany and the weather remained poor, however I had to take back what I had been thinking of those who had sent me here. We took a drive along to Frenchman's Bay, luckily there weren't any about, and we stopped once or twice along the way. The scenery was just stunning. The sea goes from a very deep, dark blue with white caps to an almost luminous sky blue, before turning brilliant white as it breaks onto the rocks and beach. The waves were around two metres high and, although I didn't see any, there are warnings of occasional freak waves coming ashore and the danger that presents. There were rocky cliffs in places with blowholes, a deep cleft cut into the cliff by the sea and wind, and what they have called the Natural Bridge. This is where the elements have literally carved away the granite in front, behind and under some of the rock to form a bridge from one escarpment to another. This whole area takes natural beauty to another level.

Just two miles away on the opposite side of the headland is King George Sound and here the sea was very calm. Whaling was a major industry there in years past and they have turned the old whaling station into a tourist spot with explanations of everything that went on. True to my previous observation about the Australians, they have also turned the local wind farm into a tourist attraction! In the UK there are groups trying to curb the spread of these structures, but perhaps English Heritage should take a leaf out of the Australian book.

We moved on some three hundred miles along the coast to Esperance. En route we ran out of petrol and three vehicles came along, each one stopping to make sure I was alright. This is the norm in Australia where, partly because of the extreme distances and partly the sparse population, everyone looks out for everybody else. I refuelled from one of my jerry cans and made a mental note that the fuel gauge should not be relied on, however there could be another problem with the fuel supply but I was not sure. After covering around two hundred miles the engine started to misfire and occasionally backfire but there was nothing visual, that I could detect, to cause it. On arriving in Esperance I again checked the engine and found that a damper on one of the carburettors was unscrewed, so I reinserted it after adding some oil and screwed it down tight. Hopefully that would resolve the matter.

I now had a sample of the type of driving that I had been told about, with absolutely straight roads for as far as you can see. At one point I stopped on top of a small hill and the road stretched as far as I could see in front and behind me. Away in the distance I could see two cars, well spaced out, but the thought that went through my head was "Traffic's building up, maybe it's rush hour!"

The South Coast Highway is flanked for much of its length by bush. This, in some ways, is similar to heathland in the UK but the vegetation tends to be between four and five feet tall, with some trees of up to ten to twelve feet.

Esperance is a seaside resort that earns most of its income from tourists. However, it also has a small, diverse and busy port exporting grain, nickel and iron ore, and importing fuel and fertilisers. The area is renowned for its pristine beaches and I decided to explore the Cape Le Grand National Park. Apart from visiting one of the beaches, where the colour of the sea is much as I described in Albany and the sand is almost white, I also went walking and climbed Frenchman's Peak. This towering granite hill affords fantastic views over the whole of the surrounding countryside and coast.

From here we would go and explore the Nullarbor Plain to Adelaide. I was surprised to hear how many Australians have never driven 'the Nullarbor' and it made me wonder what I was getting into.

We left Esperance, Western Australia at around eight in the morning. A little way out of town and we turned right onto the Eyre Highway, which would take us across the Nullarbor Plain.

Unfortunately Bridget still had a problem, which I was fairly certain was a partial blockage in the fuel system. I had given considerable consideration to whether I should sort it before leaving or to hope it would clear itself and, if not, then locating the source of the problem and clearing it. I had already checked the carburettor that had the loose damper, but that was clean, so I suspected either the hoses leading to the filter or the fuel pump. We would drive on for now.

Originally I thought this part of the journey would take two days but then I discovered the distance is one thousand four hundred miles, so three days would be more relaxed. I had several comments made to me about this route, varying from "it's very boring" to "you'll love it", along with the usual warnings about 'roos (kangaroos) and road trains. Only road trains of up to thirty-six metres may use this particular highway, (that is eleven times longer than Bridget), the really big ones are not permitted.

I quickly discovered that Bridget's engine ran fine up to fifty miles an hour after which it coughed and spluttered dreadfully and so I restricted our speed to that, or at least that is what the speedometer was telling me. However, it may have been a little inaccurate as hardly anything caught up with us. The weather had improved considerably and I had put the roof down.

I can understand the variance in the comments that I received about this route as the road is the same for mile after mile. It is flanked on both sides for most of its entirety by bush, but it does offer more variety than suggested. Sometimes it is heavily wooded, with trees twenty-five feet tall that have all of their foliage on the ends of the branches and none at all lower down. This leaves all of the lower part of the tree bare and looking spindly. Then there is bush that has densely populated shrubs of between twelve inches and eight feet in height. It is this type of cover that makes the kangaroos such a danger as it is impossible to see them until they break cover, often by jumping into the road. Finally there is the type of bush that looks very similar to British heath-land, with short, course grass and occasional small shrubs. Also, in each variety of bush there is a sprinkling of brilliantly coloured flowers.

The road is single carriageway with gravel hard shoulders either side of about seven feet each. After the first one hundred and fifty miles it suddenly changed, in that the hard shoulders became three times wider. There were also strange white painted markings across the width of the road and then I saw a sign that read 'RFDS Emergency Aircraft Runway'. They cleverly turn the road into a runway for the Australian Flying Doctor Service. I saw this no less than five times on this highway, which gives you some idea of the distances involved.

I was still taking in how far it was possible to see down the road in front of us when I saw another sign, this one stating that this was the start of Australia's longest continuous straight road, covering a distance of ninety miles. I was astounded, firstly by the length of the road where the only bend was due to the earth's curvature, and secondly that nobody had setup a tourist toll booth. (I bet there's one there next week). For a few moments I thought of doing a Mr Bean and tying off the steering so I could retire to a good book, but then I remembered the wandering menagerie and decided I should stay alert and in control!

My first night was spent in a roadhouse in Cocklebiddy that displayed a welcome sign reproduced below:

Welcome to Cocklebiddy

| | | |
|---|---|---|
| Population: | ~~10~~ 9 | People |
| | 4 | Dogs |
| | 12 | Canaries |
| | 3 | Quail |
| | 1,318,472 | Kangaroos |

(I thought about asking for a re-count.) There are many localities like this all along the highway and because of the isolation they have some unusual systems, e.g. if they have an item they want delivered to a location east of their location they merely ask a passing trucker if he would take it. There is no mobile telephone coverage in these areas because the cost of installing equipment for so few people would never be recovered. Neither are there any internet services available for travellers, although some of the roadhouses had dial-up connection for themselves.

Our second night was spent in Penong. The first thing I discovered was that we had come through two time zones and I had to put my watch forward by one and a half hours, putting me ten and a half hours ahead of the UK. Here I stayed in the local pub, only because there was no roadhouse available you understand.

I am clearly not the only person with time on their hands and an unusual sense of humour. Along the Nullarbor I spied a hat tree (lots of different coloured hats hanging from various branches), a shoe tree, that is a tree with lots of shoes not a… oh what the heck you know what I mean, a glove tree and a bottle tree. The road eventually joins the highway from Woomera and a little way down that I saw an eight foot high flying saucer, and on the other side of the road an even taller cyberman, and the pubs weren't even open. Woomera was of course the site of the British Atom bomb testing back in the 1950s. I think we may have tried to launch a number of our unique British space rockets there as well. They were unique in that they all tried tunnelling to space.

I passed through a small town called Lockiel that is beside a large lake and some wag has built a 'Nessie' look alike in the water. Just down the road is a shopping centre called Dublin's and there is a picture of a leprechaun with an Aussie cork hat.

During this type of journey my mind wanders through all sorts of things, many inconsequential, but I do find many of the place names in Australia distracting, e.g. Grasspatch, Quorn and Iron Knob. Schoolboy sense of humour aside I find the Australian tendency to give something a name that is descriptive quite refreshing. The Bottle Brush flower, the town Grasspatch is little more than just that, and the Twenty-Eight parrot that has a call that sounds like "Twenty-Eight".

By the end of Tuesday, the third day crossing the plains, we arrived in Adelaide. Bridget once again triumphed over adversity and I decided to call for assistance the next morning. I suspected that there was a blockage, possibly in the fuel tank, but we would get expert advice. We had completed one thousand, four hundred and thirty-two miles during the past three days, taking our total in Australia to date to over two thousands.

I made contact with Bob Bazzica who owns MG Sales & Service in Adelaide. Having explained the problem I was having he said to come over when I was ready and they would take a look. From the outset Bob said he was doubtful that the problem was a blockage in the tank although he, and several others, were eventually proved wrong. He wasn't happy with the amount of fuel that the mechanical pump was passing and said that really I should have an electric pump that performed better in the heat of Australia and to keep the mechanical one for emergencies. This I agreed to and he fitted the new pump. He then went on to examine the twin SU carburettors and immediately found a strong contender for the likely main cause of the trouble; one of the air filters had been put on upside down. The back plate of the filter was blocking two air holes. I didn't think it important enough to mention that the assembly of the filters was down to me, so I just shook my head and tut-tutted!

On removing the carburettor needles he also found, first, that the jet of one was protruding far too much when it really should be flush, and secondly, there were signs of wear on the needles. We agreed to order a new pair from Sydney that would be delivered the next day and Bob re-assembled the existing ones temporarily. I took the car for a test drive and after several miles of really smooth motoring was surprised when the engine suddenly backfired, followed by a complete loss of power and Bridget ground to a halt.

After allowing the engine to cool for around an hour I nursed her back to the garage. Bob said that probably there was too much fuel now being delivered to the chambers and so set up the carburettors all over again. This did the trick and the next morning the new needles were delivered, fitted and the engine tuned. The difference was palpable and even the idling speed, which had given me trouble ever since I bought the car, was now as recommended.

Bob is a member of the MG Car Club of South Australia and he invited me to meet more of the members on Friday night. They have a very good venue with all the facilities necessary. As I had come to expect in Australia, everyone gave me a very warm welcome.

Meanwhile I had been looking around Adelaide which is a very clean, open and well planned city, with lots of beautifully kept parks. It has its share of both 19th century and modern architecture, with some wonderful buildings dating back to the mid/late 19th century. One of these is the town hall and another the General Post Office. I noticed one of the foundation stones of the Post Office building was engraved with the words "This stone was laid by HRH Duke of Edinburgh 1868". I really didn't realise he was as old as that. It explains a lot.

We left Adelaide Saturday morning and set course for Geelong. I had decided to take the advice of several people and follow the Princes Highway to Port Fairy and then the Great Ocean Highway.

The journey was uneventful and, not wanting to drive too far on the first day after Bridget's repairs, we stopped for the night at Mt Gambier.

The following day we left at nine o'clock and continued towards Port Fairy. The countryside around there is far more cultivated than any I had seen before and the animals to be avoided on the road now included Koalas. So far I had seen very few animals of any type although there was plenty of evidence at the side of the roads of kangaroos killed by traffic, mainly at night, I was told.

Bridget was driving well, with no signs of any of her previous troubles and we were cruising quite happily at seventy miles per hour. I kept an eye out on all of the trees at the roadside, hoping to see a koala, and also had half an eye on the road in case of anything else. Rounding a bend I thought I saw something in a tree on the right and turned my head to get a better look and of course when I turned back, there in the middle of the road was a koala. Bridget's brakes were functioning well! We stopped just short of the koala that just sat staring at us. With what can only be described as a look of disdain the koala got up and meandered off towards the bushes. I was panicking trying to get my camera out of its bag and haul myself out of the car, but by that time the koala was climbing quite high up a tree and choosing which leaves would taste best. However, I managed to get a couple of shots.

Driving along the Great Ocean Highway is a marvellous experience. It is not just the beautiful seascapes but also the surrounding countryside, some of it is Australian bush, lots of tropical rain forest, and some which could easily be confused with Sussex.

We stopped at several look-out points to view some of the unusual rocky outcrops carved by the sea, such as London Bridge, the Razorback and the Arch. The blue of the sea all along this stretch of coast is almost luminous, and the waves make for great surfing off the beaches. Over the years there have been many sea tragedies and locally it has become known as The Shipwreck Coast.

I had met a 'bloke' called Rob whilst I was in Adelaide and he told me of a number of places to go in the area if I liked walking. He also drew a 'mud map' for me and I decided to stop at Lorne and go off on one of these excursions. I visited the Erskine Falls, which is a delightful spot, and then walked through some of the rainforest.

We arrived in Geelong at approximately five o'clock. My intention was to stay for a week and explore nearby places, including, of course, Melbourne.

Geelong is a small town approximately thirty-five miles from Melbourne. It is built on the hills running down to Corio Bay and has a classic English style seaside resort pier. It was once dependant on the wool trade and there is now a museum telling the detailed story. There is a good selection of wineries, as there had been in almost every town and city we had visited in Australia so far.

I made contact with the MG Car Club the first morning after my arrival and as at previous towns they were tremendous. I had dinner with John and Sandra Bennett the first evening. John was President of the club.

It was arranged for Bridget to lead a gala procession on Saturday as a guest of honour. This is an annual fundraising event for the local hospital. I thought it would be a good idea to get some signs for Bridget so that people would at least have an idea what we were about. John immediately contacted Peter Smith, who was liaising with the gala organisers on behalf of the MG club, and in no time at all Peter had arranged for a company to make the signage for me. So Bridget now had the web address on either side of her body (sounds as if she had tattoos) and signs saying "Round the World Drive" on both bumpers.

The official organisers also contacted me and arranged for the local press to do a photo shoot and interview with me, so we got some good exposure for UNICEF.

I extended our stay in Geelong by two days as there was an MG club event on Wednesday 26th November and I had been invited to meet many more of the members there.

Melbourne is a busy and apparently thriving metropolis. Like the other cities so far visited, it has a mixture of Victorian (the period not the state), Georgian, colonial and contemporary architecture. There are several notable buildings: the Eureka Skydeck, the State Library, the state of Victoria's Parliament House, the Gothic Bank and Stock Exchange and the Shot Tower. The last of those listed was a lead pipe and shot factory that the authorities wanted to preserve but was in the way of a new retail development. With the usual Aussie adaptability they built the retail development around the old factory, producing a building within a building. They'll never need to worry about the roof leaking! Additionally, there are a host of church buildings, some dating back to the mid eighteen hundreds. The city boasts its own 'Eye', similar to the one in London, and has reintroduced trams.

Saturday, and the weather looked bleak for the gala. However, the rain stopped long enough for the procession to go ahead in the dry, even if the wind was a little blustery. Bridget led eighteen other MGs, which carried some of Australia's Beijing Olympians and Para-Olympians. Afterwards I was treated to a typical 'Aussie Barbie' where I had the chance to meet more of the MG club members.

The weather in Victoria was anything but typical, with heavy rain and strong winds. The Victoria Alps even had a snowfall during the week. Later I was to find out that this was the southern edge of a severe weather system centred over Brisbane in Queensland. They suffered some flooding and buildings were damaged by the storms.

The weather cleared up early in the week and on Tuesday I returned to Lorne to go walking in the rainforest again. I had a tourist map and set out along the Garvey track, making for the Sheoak Falls. However, the map was a little misleading and I was some three miles past the location of the falls when I came to Sharps Track. I was now 'off the map' but used some logic and followed the Sharps Track, believing it would take me back to my starting point eventually. This proved to be correct but instead of a relaxing five mile walk I completed a slightly more tiring eleven miles.

Whilst in the rainforest I came across an animal with a strong resemblance to a hedgehog except that it was much larger, with long black spines tipped with yellow. I was told that this was a spiky anteater, proper name, Echidnas. Amongst all the greens, browns and greys of the forest vegetation there are constant flashes of brilliant red, and blue caused by parrots in flight, but they proved very difficult to photograph as they wouldn't stay still long enough.

On my last day in Geelong I was honoured to be a guest of the MG club at their Christmas bash. They presented me with a club cap, jacket and, very kindly, a donation for UNICEF. Sometimes it can be very difficult leaving places when you have been made to feel like you belong.

Rather than taking the major highway north all round Melbourne I decided we would go down to Queenscliff and take the ferry to

Sorrento. From there we could pick up the South Gippsland Highway and eventually the Princes Highway, keeping close to the coast all the way to Sydney.

After a reasonable breakfast and a chin wag with the motel owner we set off to Queenscliff, arriving just in time... to watch the stern of the boat moving off from the jetty. We would have to wait for an hour for the next boat. Finally, at nine o'clock, we were aboard and on our way. We had Port Phillip Bay on one side and the Bass Straits on the other. I left Bridget on the car deck and went up to the first passenger deck to watch the dolphins. A pod was playing in the ship's wake all the way over to Sorrento and they were fascinating to observe.

Bridget's new signs were garnering attention and several people had come over during the day and asked where we started from, which countries had we been to, etc.

From Sorrento we made our way through Flinders, Hastings, then down to Korumburra and Leongatha. I decided we should stop for petrol in Leongatha and just as we did Bridget's engine almost died on me. I wasn't sure what the problem was, but it wasn't petrol as we still had around a quarter of a tank full. Anyway, I pulled up to a pump and got out of the car. The attendant was talking to another customer who looked over and having seen the new signs on the bumpers, said, "How far have you driven so far?" I told him, his facial expression changed and he said, "Oh you're serious." We then chatted for a couple of minutes and he went on his way. I filled the tank and went into the station to pay. The attendant asked, "Have you got some time to spare?" I replied that I could take half an hour and he told me that he had rung the local newspaper whilst I was filling the car and they wanted to interview me if I had time, and could I pop up to their office. It was only two minutes away and so I duly did an interview and a quick photo shoot for them.

After all the excitement I had forgotten that Bridget's engine had almost stalled at the garage and we went on our way. After about twenty minutes I suddenly noticed the needle of the temperature gauge was almost in the danger area so I slowed down and the engine almost stalled. I maintained a steady forty miles an hour and the temperature gradually dropped but as soon as I increased the speed it rose rapidly again. We pulled into a public barbeque area and after the engine had cooled for half an hour I checked the water level. Sure enough it needed filling, which I did. That appeared to have been the problem and the remainder of the journey was uneventful.

We arrived at Lakes Entrance at just after four in the afternoon and found a motel. The town is a pretty holiday resort with an apparently healthy fishing industry. There are several sea water lakes that make for a picture postcard landscape with an interesting bird population. I walked down to one of the many pontoons where the fishing boats, and some private yachts, are moored and there were seven pelicans preening themselves and generally taking life easy. On land these are quite comical, ungainly birds but in the air they glide with poise, although looking almost pre-historic.

Friday morning and we set off towards Sydney, although I didn't expect to reach there until the following day. Once again we drove through a lot of forested areas bordering the coast with glimpses of the sea seen through occasional breaks in the trees. Sometimes the forest gave way to beautiful rolling green hills on the landward side, very reminiscent of the UK.

Late morning and we arrived at the town of Eden. Like Lakes Entrance, this is a resort town and a great deal of pride is taken in its appearance. Eden is also a centre for whale enthusiasts with a Killer Whale Museum. Most of the whales seen in the bay, however, are humpbacks and unfortunately most had left by mid-November so I didn't see any.

I thought I heard a screeching noise from Bridget several times en route and did a check to see if anything was visibly wrong. There appeared to be some oil leaking from one of the wheels and so I jacked the car up in the middle of Eden's main street! Once I had removed the wheel it was apparent that the 'leak' was no more than some grease from the hub that had liquidised due to the heat and escaped from the hub cover. Everything else was fine and later in the day, having heard the noise several more times, I decided to stop. Then I heard the noise again and realised that I had been fooled by some Australian bird with a screeching call. Although relieved, I was not amused.

Once again Bridget's engine overheated even though the water and oil levels were fine. I was beginning to wonder if the water pump was sticking as the temperature would suddenly climb and then recede again. I could not think of anything else at that moment and I didn't think it was just hard work in high temperatures because she had coped with that well in both Pakistan and India.

We spent the night at Bateman's Bay, yet another of the numerous coastal towns but we were now in New South Wales, having crossed the border early in the afternoon. Again, picturesque, with the River Clyde running under an interesting bridge before emptying into the bay. The bridge consists of five steel truss spans and one opening truss span of the vertical lift type. The opening lift span is ninety feet long and can be lifted seventy-five feet. A sign said it was officially opened in November 1956; I guess they meant the bridge was open for use then, not the span...

The penultimate day of November 2008 and we arrived in Sydney. The last two hundred miles from Bateman's Bay were straightforward until the final five miles when once again Bridget's engine spluttered and almost stalled. I managed to coax her over to the side of the road for a visual check and I removed, cleaned and checked the points. I still believed there was some sort of problem with the fuel supply. After allowing the engine to cool for half an hour she started up again and we continued to the Sydney Olympic Park, where I checked into a hotel. I knew I must resolve the problem whilst I was there.

On my first full day in Sydney I was invited to attend the Tasman

Revival Race meeting. This meeting is an annual event marking the races that took place in the 1960s and in particular the period when Jack Brabham was at the peak of his racing career.

There were many excellent cars both on display and racing but for me the pièce de résistance was not one, but two genuine D-Type Jaguars. There are only fifty-four known surviving models of this classic racing car and they are worth in the order of two million pounds each.

The next day, as Bridget was not running well, I, with the able assistance of Lindsay Trevitt, the President of the Sydney MG Car Club, removed the petrol tank and checked it for blockages. It appeared to be fine, but later in the day Bridget stopped running altogether and left me standing at the side of the road. After half an hour things seemed to settle down again and she started up and took me home perfectly.

On Tuesday I did the official tourist bit, visiting the city centre (CBT) and sights such as the Sydney Harbour Bridge, the Opera House and several other locations. The city doesn't appear to have quite as many colonial buildings as some other cities although Government House, St Mary's Cathedral and the Chelsea Barracks building are worth a look. There are also several old churches. There is a definite vibrancy about Sydney and it's positively exciting.

Bridget continued to have running problems and with the help of Stuart Ratcliff, owner of the MG Centre of Sydney, the SU carburettors were checked again, the new fuel pump was replaced with another and re-sited to the rear of the car close to the petrol tank and replacement fuel lines were installed. There was definitely a problem, with the fuel flow stopping completely from time to time, and it left us to consider the petrol tank once again. It was then that Stuart suggested that the damage caused when we were driven off the road in India could be to blame. The severe dent received on the petrol tank was right on the well area where the fuel pick-up was and it might well have been damaged causing intermittent blockages to occur. A new tank would be sourced on Monday and I made a mental note to trust my initial instincts more in future.

Stuart also discovered that the compression of cylinders one and four was considerably higher than two and three, which could be indicative of early head gasket failure. I would have to consider replacing it when we got to the Gold Coast.

On Sunday I was invited to join the Sydney MG Car Club Christmas breakfast run. This took us to Mittagong, some fifty kilometres south of Sydney, and afterwards Lindsay showed me some of the forest and countryside areas around Fitzroy Falls before going down to Nowra.

Bridget's fuel supply problem had now been fixed, or so I thought. As well as replacing the fuel tank we also replaced the narrow bore copper feed pipe with braided rubber piping. We drove north to Woy Woy as a check on everything and although the engine had been smoother in the past it should be fine for the drive to Gold Coast. We stopped briefly at Kariong to check the fuel flow and within two minutes a four-by-four had stopped beside us to chat. The occupants were a charming couple visiting from the Brisbane area and after hearing what I was doing they made an impromptu donation to UNICEF.

On the way back to Sydney I saw a car, just a short distance ahead of us, suddenly pull into the side of the highway and stop. As we drew alongside I could see it was a young lady and her car clearly had a puncture. I steered Bridget in front of her car, stopped and offered to help. It transpired that the lady had only bought the car a week earlier and when we looked in the boot there was no jack or wheel brace. We borrowed Bridget's tools and changed the wheel, although well outside Formula One's standard eight second time for a pit stop. It was nice to be able to pay back some of the assistance proffered to us by all the MG clubs in this country.

The last day of our stay in Sydney and I took Bridget to see the iconic Bondi Beach. I wasn't sure what to expect as I had received varying reports about the place and I am glad my expectations were not too high. The suburb of Bondi is not as vibrant and exciting as St Kilda in Melbourne but it has to be said that the bay is superb. Nowhere near as big as I had imagined, it's about the same size as the beach at Weymouth in the UK, but the colour of the sea and the 'rollers' are quite spectacular. Also, of course, it is in very close proximity to Sydney City Centre.

Next we would head off towards the Gold Coast and Brisbane.

Leaving the Sydney suburb of Ashfield early in the morning I had hoped to miss the rush of traffic to the city but to no avail, as there was an accident holding up all the early commuters on the highway. As we inched towards the junction with the main freeway towards Brisbane I became aware of someone calling out from another vehicle. It had also become clear that the Australians are extremely supportive of individuals attempting unusual tasks and Bridget's bumper stickers declaring "Round the World Drive" had drawn his attention.

The voice calling out belonged to Ade Kass, a fellow Brit working in Australia. He's a lovely chap, but with the unfortunate condition of being a Liverpool football supporter. He noted the web site address and contacted me again later that day. I tried several times to encourage people through the web site to give us a toot on their horn or to come over and say "G'day".

We drove to Port Macquarie, just two hundred and twenty miles north of Sydney, and stopped for the night. Bridget's engine handled the journey without trouble. We were in no rush as were not expected on the Gold Coast until Sunday, giving us three days of gentle motoring.

The names of almost all the places, rivers and even every creek I found beguiling, such as Coolangolook, Pete's Crossing, Wally's Place, Bowling Alley Point and Bald Knob Creek. I'd love to know the stories or characters behind many of these.

From Port Macquarie we ventured on to Ballina, following the

Pacific Highway. After about an hour of motoring I noticed that Bridget's oil pressure was abnormally low. I pulled into a service station and checked under the bonnet to find, oil had been escaping from the filler cap on-top of the rocker cover. On removing and examining it I could see that the rubber seal was in poor condition. I didn't have one with me so I would need to source one during our stay on the Gold Coast. I added a litre of oil to the engine and we continued on our way. I also detected a noticeable improvement in the fuel consumption since changing the tank, feed pipe and pump.

We drove to Ballina the next day, another two hundred and twenty miles, passing through Coffs Harbour, where I had originally thought of staying. I changed my mind about staying only because we had arrived very early and I was enjoying the drive, so I took a quick look around then got back into the car.

From Ballina we made our way to Tweed Heads, one of the Twin Towns, the other being Coolangatta. Although these two towns run into each other building wise, the state border of New South Wales and Queensland divides them. Back in history this was an important demarcation as slave workers in the sugar cane industry of Queensland were able to escape to New South Wales, where slavery was outlawed, and gain their freedom.

There is a tourist lookout point above Tweed Heads that offers an excellent view across the Heads, down the Tweed Valley and over to Mount Warning. Although I have made occasional critical remarks about the Australian tourist industry trying to make attractions out of nothing, they are extremely good at locating lookouts all over the country that are excellent areas for tourists to take a break and see some of the natural beauty surrounding them (English Tourist Board take note).

Sunday 14th December and we met up with Gary Lock and several members of the Gold Coast MG Car Club near Danger Point, which overlooks Coolangatta Beach. Gary had been emailing me since the start of the run, having seen a magazine article about it, and had invited me to stay with him and his wife, Anita. We were later joined by a Channel Nine television news team that had been arranged courtesy of Gary, and, by pure chance, a reporter and photographer from the local paper, the *Bulletin*. They arrived at the spot to cover another story but on seeing Bridget, did an impromptu interview.

The time had arrived for Bridget to have her engine inspected for outstanding problems. I knew that the seal on the oil filler cap was leaking and needed to be replaced but there was more serious concern about what was going on inside the engine. We checked the compression in Sydney and the pressures were, from cylinder one to four in order, one hundred and fifty, ninety, one hundred, one hundred and fifty. It might just be the head gasket or a valve but could of course be the rings or something even more serious.

I visited Brian Darke, who is another of Australia's gurus on MGs. He immediately confirmed the compression reading and sent me to a garage in the Palm Beach area. Here, under the expert eye of Andrew Allen, owner of the Sixth Avenue Garage, I removed the cylinder head. There was nothing visibly wrong with the gasket and so we sent the head off to be vacuum checked. It transpired that two of the valves needed to be ground and the valve followers replaced. I re-fitted the head using a new gasket and Andrew checked the valve clearances.

Bridget now sounded and ran very well. There were two minor things to be fixed, the first was the tick-over which was too fast, caused, we thought, by wear on the accelerator spindle either preventing the carburettors returning to the stop position or allowing air to infiltrate one of the carburettors, hence affecting the mixture. The second problem was that the seal on the oil filler cap needed to be replaced but we didn't have a spare. As neither of these were 'show stoppers' I decided I would fix them later.

We were now ready to continue our adventure but first we had Christmas and New Year to celebrate. It seemed strange to see all the decorations and lights and to hear carols being sung whilst outside the temperature was thirty five degrees centigrade.

Millions of people around the world believe that Christmas should be a special time, and so it proved on Australia's Gold Coast.

It started when I received a message, via our Bridget the Midget website, which said, "I have just been reading in the local press about your adventure and may be able to help you." This transpired to be the article resulting from our unscheduled interview with the *Bulletin* news reporter when we arrived on the Gold Coast.

Ah, I thought, another willing MG-head offering me possible solutions to Bridget's mechanical problems, but they don't know that I have already resolved them. I will call this chap and have a chat and thank him for his trouble. I tried calling the number he had left for me but there was no answer so I decided to leave it until later as I needed to do a couple of tasks and then get ready to go out for the evening. Gary and Anita Lock were taking me out for dinner that evening so I didn't want to be late.

I spent a very pleasant day with some other MG members showing me around the area and generally entertaining me (what a life) and I didn't have the opportunity to try calling my mystery person until returning to the Lock's home. I decided to try calling once more before going for a shower and getting dressed for dinner. That sounds a lot grander than was the case, because when you are travelling for eighteen months in a sports car there is little room for a dinner jacket.

The phone was answered.

"Hello, Mark Thomas."

"Hello Mark, this is Roy Locock from the Bridget the Midget driving challenge."

"Oh hello, Roy, thanks for calling me, I think I may be able to help you with some fundraising."

This was totally unexpected as I hadn't for one moment thought of the 'help' being offered as being for the fundraising effort. To date, most of the donations received had been as the direct result of MG enthusiasts' assistance and generosity.

Mark continued, "I am on the Gold Coast currently with a show at Conrad Jupiter's Casino called Abba Mania. I was reading in the local press about your round the world adventure, which I happen to think is pretty impressive. You probably know that the royalties for the recording of Abba's song 'Chiquitita' were donated to UNICEF and we would like to include the song in the show, then introduce you and have a bucket collection as the audience leaves at the end. What do you think?"

What did I think! My mind was running at half speed; was this real?

"I would be delighted Mark," I said, "When did you have in mind?"

"What are you doing tonight?"

Ah, I thought, I knew there would be a catch, as I was going out with Gary and Anita. I wondered if I could do it later in the week or if they would understand and be prepared to change the arrangement. I told Mark that I had the prior engagement but that I would speak to the people involved and see what could be worked out. He immediately extended an offer to give them seats at the show if they wished to come along.

I should have known that they would immediately agree to change our plans and go along to the theatre. I called Mark back and we arranged to meet at the theatre shortly after seven that evening, he had already got the theatre management's agreement to the changes that would be needed and to do a collection.

Our tickets were waiting for us at the box office when we arrived. I was briefly taken back stage to meet Mark before the show got under way and he briefed me as to what would happen. Mark wrote this Abba tribute show back in 1998 and has been presenting and performing in it around the world ever since.

The moment came during the number 'Dancing Queen' when I was taken back stage ready to be introduced to the audience. Mark was very gracious in his description of what I was doing and most importantly explained that I was raising funds for UNICEF. After I had been up on stage they played the 'Chiquitita' number and the audience loved it. As I always found in Australia, the generosity of the people is fantastic and they donated over seven hundred and fifty dollars. As if that wasn't enough, Mark immediately offered to make it up to the round thousand from his own pocket.

This was the best possible Christmas gift that I, or UNICEF, could have asked for and it came about in such an unexpected way. I felt it reflected the true spirit of the season.

Before leaving Queensland's Gold Coast I visited several places where forest walks are common. There is nothing common, however, about the scenery and I experienced some beautiful views around Springbrook National Park and glimpsed some of Australia's wildlife that I had not previously seen. This included a Lace monitor, a type of lizard, which was crossing the road as I returned to base. The reptile was over three feet long and had green bands around its body. I have never seen a lizard this size before and at first it seemed almost as big as the car. I thought for a moment it would mistake Bridget for another monitor and either attack her or try to mate!

I had arranged to meet some members of the Queensland Sprite Car Club, based in Brisbane, on the way through the area and join them at a 'Barbie'. I was amazed when around twenty-five people turned up at very short notice, just a couple of days after Christmas, to meet me and talk about my adventures. Just like the MG clubs before them, they were extremely welcoming and curious to see what sort of person takes on a challenge that pushes at the boundaries of the capabilities of a British sports car. They also brought a terrific display of Sprite cars, including an iconic 'Bug-eye'.

The following day Bridget and I drove to Noosa Heads, on the

Sunshine Coast. My neighbours from Chinnor in England moved to Australia in August 2007 and now live in Noosa. Mike and Tricia Fairburn took their MGB GT with them and I promised to visit, even though Mike thought I would never make it. This is the Mike that had helped me re-cover the seats when I was rebuilding Bridget.

Whilst in Noosa I was also lucky enough to meet Graham and Sheila Peters who invited me to join them for lunch along with Phil Evett. Graham is the President of the Sunshine Coast MG Car Club and Phil is the club Secretary. They were disappointed that I wasn't staying longer and able to attend a club meeting but the road to Port Douglas, north of Cairns, was beckoning and I really had to get going.

Everyone kept telling me that we should have gone the other direction around the country, therefore visiting Darwin in the Northern Territory first. The reason was that January is the beginning of the wet season and also when typhoons hit the area. There was a very real chance that we would be confronted by flooding and Bridget was unable to swim, in fact she could only safely paddle in water less than six inches deep.

The journey north entailed two one-night stopovers and advanced me by some one thousand two hundred miles. To put that in context it is the equivalent of driving from London to Glasgow each day for three days. Bridget found the first day hard going in the thirty-five degree heat and so the next two days I reduced our cruising speed to around fifty-five miles per hour. We were losing a little oil from the filler cap still but the engine was running well.

Whilst in Port Douglas I decided to do the normal tourist bit and take a river trip up the Dickson Inlet to see some of the local wildlife. We spotted a couple of crocodiles hiding at the side of the water amongst the mangrove roots. There was also some interesting birdlife, including a majestic sea eagle.

The following day I went out to the Great Barrier Reef for some snorkelling. I was told there was no need to look out for sharks as the 'crocs' had eaten them all. So as long as the Box jellyfish had stung all the sea kraits it would be relatively safe! The reef is absolutely beautiful and well worth the effort to get there. The different shapes and colours of the coral and plant life are stunning, as are the thousands of different fish.

Then the time arrived to start the trek to Darwin that everyone had said could be difficult. I now had one twenty litre jerry can full of fuel and another containing water. The water tank I had wrapped in cooking foil to try to keep the temperature low. I didn't know if it would work or not but it was worth trying and, as it transpired, it worked well. Typically, the effort was then wasted as it started to rain.

We drove south through Mareeba to The Lynd Junction. It was my intention to then drive on to Hughenden but Bridget needed fuel so we stopped at a filling station. I decided to have a coffee and whilst drinking it a fellow traveller came in and, walking up to me, asked, "Is that your MG outside?" When I said "Yes" he asked where I was headed and so I told him. "Not today you're not, I've just come along that road in my Land Cruiser and the route is flooded to a depth of about three feet. There is no way that you will get through." I had a feeling of deja vu but realised that this advice was more informed than that which I had received on the Iranian/Pakistan border. So I decided we would drop down to Charters Towers and then turn west on the highway A6 to Mount Isa.

Some forty-five miles south of The Lynd Junction I rounded a bend and the whole road was awash. One of the creeks had risen above the flood level, only by about eight inches but it was still rising and flowing very fast. I decided to risk a crossing, my main concern being washed off the road more than anything else. Bridget made it quite easily, helped by the extra weight on her rear axle from the fuel and water. The most worrying thing was that the creek level had risen to the flood level in less than thirty minutes and there was still plenty of rain about. The whole area is very flat and widespread flooding was possible.

Having arrived in Charters Towers, a little tired, I decided to watch the local news and heard that the whole area from Julia Creek to Mount Isa was impassable and the police had asked people not to attempt to drive through there. We would have to wait and see what developed. The following day I spoke to the Mount Isa police and was advised not to attempt the journey. The rain was the heaviest it had been for several years and one car had already been swept off the road the previous day. Fortunately the occupants were rescued. I would just have to wait.

Charters Towers is a small gold mining town, established in the mid 19th century. The mines all closed down when the seams ran out in the early 20th century but many of the buildings have been lovingly preserved and restored where necessary. Not surprisingly there is a mining museum and a number of tourist attractions centred around those times. Included in these is the Stock Exchange, established to curtail mining stock scams that flourished for a time, and there are a number of interesting stories about prospectors, mine claims and claim jumping. The town was wealthy and boasted good educational services, including its own School of Mines, gas street lighting in 1888, and its own medical facilities. In its heyday it became known as 'The World'.

I started my second day here running half way around 'The World', and that before breakfast! My fitness level was woeful and I needed to shape up.

I had plenty of time to take in this interesting period of local history whilst waiting for the road from Charters Towers to Mount Isa to re open, following what transpired to be the worst floods for more than thirty years. Even when the water subsided and the road at Julia Creek and Cloncurry re opened, I was not able to proceed further than Mount Isa as a large part of the road from Isa to Camooweal had been washed away and needed to be rebuilt. The delay would be over four weeks, or more if there was further significant rainfall. I was, however, impressed that the authorities expected to rebuild the route in such a short period as in the UK they would take four years just to decide who would pay for it.

On my third day there the first cyclone of the season formed in the Gulf of Carpentaria and delivered deluges of rain. Some places had over four hundred millimetres in twenty-four hours! Locally there was concern that the River Burdekin would overflow. I crossed over the bridge and saw that the river level was about twenty-five feet below the bridge but within forty-eight hours the level was lapping at the edge of the road. Things change so rapidly there and the volume of water is almost unbelievable. In 1946 the level rose over sixty feet.

Things were starting to mount up as there was also an outbreak of dengue fever in Townsville, which at about one hundred and fifty kilometres away, is only just down the road.

Charters Towers does have other problems, specifically a flock of over fifty thousand flying foxes, or fruit bats as they are commonly called. They swarm to this green oasis, in an otherwise arid countryside, and roost in all the tall trees. They are protected and therefore there is nothing that can be done to persuade them to move on. They do present a public health risk in the same way that pigeons do in European cities and cause considerable crop damage on the fruit farms.

During the first weekend I drove over to Ravenswood, sixty miles east of Charters Towers. This is another gold mining town and there is still an operating open-cast mine here. The population is around two hundred and thirty today, but in its heyday it was more like five thousand. Most of the town's buildings are from the early days, although restored, and the town has been made a heritage site and listed by the National Trust. The town museum is housed in the old courthouse and has some fascinating items that demonstrate the way people lived in those early mining days.

A fortnight passed since my arrival, and the road was declared open between Charters Towers and Richmond so I decided to press on as far as possible. Just ten miles west of Charters Towers and there was plenty of evidence of the flooding. In places the water was still up to the edge of the road floodways and much of the surrounding countryside was

*Calimanesti, Romania*

*Sumela Monastery, Nr Trabzon, Turkey*

*Ishak Pasha Sarayi, Dogubayazit, Turkey*

*Fuel Stop, Esfahan, Iran*

*Iran/Pakistan Border*

*Classic Pakistani Truck*

*The Robbers Road - 400 miles of this*

*Leaving Dalbandin, Pakistan*

*Foothills Of The Himalayas, Overlooking Dharmshala*

*Rambagh Palace, Jaipur*

*Passing The Albert Hall, Jaipur*

*Suburbs of Jaipur*

*The Palace, Udaipur*

*Xmas Day, Australian Style – Gold Coast*

*'Salty' In Dickson Inlet, Port Douglas*

*Road Train At Charters Towers, Queensland*

*Flooding On Victoria Highway, Northern Territories*

*Turners River, Nr Port Headland, Western Australia*

*Argentina/Chile Border Post*

*Andes South Of Camana, Peru*

*Coast Road Nr Yauca, Peru*

*Nazca To Cusco Road*

*Over The Ecuadorian Border*

*Not The Usual Highway*

*River Border Between Honduras/Guatemala*

*Bridget On The Strip, USA*

*Kern River Canyon, California*

*Samuel H Boardman National Park, Oregon*

*If It's Asleep, Poke It With A Big Stick*

*Kettle River, Nr Nelson, British Columbia*

still under water. The scenery also changed again and for much of the journey from The Towers there was nothing obstructing the view all the way to the horizon. The whole landscape was similar to English meadows but hundreds of times bigger, with just occasional trees. What made this particular scene so unusual was the colour. Normally this is bright red, sun baked, rock hard arid countryside but because of the rains it was now green all the way.

I arrived in Richmond shortly after lunch and booked into another motel. I didn't want to stay for more than a night as it could rain again at any time and the roads in both directions could once more be cut off. The Richmond police advised me that the section of highway that was washed out at Camooweal would be passable in ten to fourteen days' time.

Bridget and I left just before eight o'clock in the morning and headed for Mount Isa by way of Julia Creek and Cloncurry. Both of these places had figured prominently in the flooding and I was a little nervous. Julia Creek is almost ninety miles west of Richmond and the journey went without event. The scenery all along the way was very different to what I had seen before, with vast areas of grasslands and very few trees or bushes.

There was plenty of evidence of the floods, however, with a considerable amount of standing water on either side, but fortunately not across the road. I decided to stop at a roadhouse just the other side of Julia Creek and asked a police officer about the conditions ahead. He said there was water across the road in several places but that it was standing, not flowing, and only fifteen centimetres deep. Bridget should be OK.

Approximately twenty miles west of Julia Creek we found the first floodwater over the road. There was a Land Cruiser coming the other way so we let it cross and I watched the level carefully to see if Bridget would be OK. I was not convinced and neither was the driver of the four by four when he saw Bridget. My main concern was the speed at which the water crossed the road because it causes a build-up against the wheels which can then wash the car off the road. The driver of the four by four offered to turn around and drive ahead, effectively making a shallow path for us to follow, but before he could do that another vehicle travelling in the same direction as me arrived and he offered to do the same thing. The other driver said he would wait until we were safely across, in case Bridget stalled and needed a tow.

So it was that we ventured through the first flood and the vehicle that shepherded us over helped at several more crossings further on. Only once did Bridget hesitate and that was when the water depth came over the front bumper but she managed to make it to the other side and after coughing and spluttering a little we were able to continue our journey to Mount Isa. Our thanks to the unknown assistant in the multi-cab ute (utility or pick-up truck).

As we arrived at Mount Isa it started raining again!

Mount Isa's main feature is somewhat unusual for the centre of a city and certainly conspicuous. It is a huge mine owned and operated by Xstrata and is one of the largest producers of copper ore in Australia.

Situated five hundred and fifty miles from Townsville, on the Queensland coast, Mount Isa has been referred to as the Oasis of the Outback. I noticed the thousands of acres of green pastureland on the journey from Charters Towers but this was very deceptive. As I commented previously, this country is normally arid, brown sun-scorched ground and was only green because of the recent rains and flooding. Many Australians have never seen it in that state.

Bridget developed a problem with the starter motor, which kept sticking, so I had to turn the rotor first with a spanner before turning the engine over in the normal way. Then on one occasion I noticed that the whole motor was loose. Trying to reach the fixing bolts was difficult and so I went to K&M Motors. Without hesitation they agreed to lift it on a hoist and tighten up the bolts. In fact they found it was not the fixing bolts that were loose but the long bolts that go right through the motor holding the total assembly together. Once tightened up things were better but I would have to lubricate the rotor when I did the next service, probably around Darwin.

I learnt on Wednesday that the road into the Northern Territory would be opened, to light traffic only, in the following two days. Traffic travelling east to west would be allowed through between eight-thirty and eleven-thirty in the morning and west to east traffic would be allowed between one-thirty and five o'clock in the afternoon. Bridget and I left Mt Isa at nine o'clock Friday morning and we were one of the first cars through. Certainly we were the first MG, probably for several years. There was still a considerable quantity of water lying at the sides of the highway and the damage to the road itself was quite extensive. The authorities were to be congratulated for getting it re-commissioned so quickly.

Again there were several locations where water was across the road but it was noticeably less than two days previous.

We arrived at Tennant Creek at around five o'clock Friday afternoon. This is approximately three hundred and fifty miles north of Alice Springs but I wouldn't have time to visit there. The next day I would drive north towards Darwin but would have to break the journey halfway. The total distance to Darwin from Tennant Creek is approximately six hundred miles. We covered four hundred and thirty miles that day and Bridget's engine was running very hot. Mind you, the air temperature was around thirty-six degrees centigrade and quite humid. I would check the oil and water levels before moving on.

I decided to get on the road early and have breakfast at a roadhouse. There was one at Three Ways Junction, just fifteen miles up the road, and whilst I was there I was told about another Englishman who was riding a small motorcycle from Sydney to Darwin and then back to England. I eventually caught up with him at another roadhouse about one hundred and thirty kilometres further on. He had a 110cc motorbike and indeed was going to ride it all the way back to the UK so we exchanged notes over coffee.

The Stuart Highway was busier than the Barkly Highway had been the previous day, when I only saw five vehicles in the two hundred kilometre stretch, but it was still very quiet compared to roads in Europe. I saw my first dingo during the afternoon; it emerged from the long grass that currently bordered both sides of the highway due to the rainfall. The vegetation increases the danger of collisions between animals and vehicles as it made it very difficult to see the beasts until they actually step into the road.

Bridget suffered a fit or something that day. I could suddenly smell petrol and pulled over to the side of the road concerned that if there was a leak, with the engine so hot it could easily ignite. When I lifted the bonnet the support arm that normally holds it up didn't move and I discovered that the bolt that held it in position had disappeared. I found another and fixed it, and sure enough there was evidence of fuel on the exterior of one of the carburettors. I switched the ignition on so that the pump would work and petrol flooded out. I thought it was a hose leaking and changed it, but the problem persisted. There is a connecting pipe between the two carburettors so I removed the far end to see if there was a blockage causing the supply to back-up. There was nothing that I could see and so I removed the carburettor float chamber. There was a slight hiss as I did so but nothing visibly wrong so I reconnected everything. After allowing the engine to cool for half an hour I started it up once again and the problem did not recur. The following day I would need to keep an eye on things but it appeared for the moment that I may have cleared an air lock or it may have been a sticking needle.

We stayed the night at Mataranka, a small community on the Stuart Highway, and the next day I hoped to make it to Darwin. I had just heard on the news that Mount Isa was again flooded and cut off.

Sunday 25th January and it was a bad start to the day. As usual I checked both the water and oil levels in Bridget's engine and topped up the oil. She was certainly either burning oil or loosing it somewhere. I broke my normal routine, which was to remove the filler cap and place it on the front bumper whilst I topped up the oil, and instead I placed it on the heater unit. My mind was not on the job and I just closed the bonnet when I had filled her and left. A mile up the road I pulled over because she sounded noisier than usual and I found the oil cap was missing. I quickly checked around the engine; not seeing it I locked the car and started walking back to the motel, searching all along the roadside as I went. I couldn't find it so I returned to the car, searching along the other side of the road. I was only too aware that as the top was round it could easily have fallen onto the road and rolled for a long way. Also there were ditches full of water that it could have rolled into. I resigned myself to having to make a temporary cover and return to the motel until I could get a replacement.

I lifted the bonnet again and looked to see if it had fallen under the car as it ground to a halt, but no such luck. Just as I was turning away I saw it lodged between the heater and the battery. I recovered and refitted it with a sigh of relief. I was annoyed with myself for being careless and thankful for that guardian angel, again. For the second time I started off on the final three hundred miles to Darwin.

Although we made good time over the first two hundred miles Bridget was clearly not running properly and stalled as soon as I slowed down at a roadhouse. I decided to leave her to cool down and got myself a coffee. Afterwards I looked under the bonnet and immediately saw that she had been leaking fuel again. I checked the points and removed each spark plug in turn. Sure enough, the plug from cylinder three had heavy soot deposits and was badly discoloured so I replaced it with another, but I feared that either the valve had given up or the piston ring was broken. By good luck a couple of bikers had been watching and came over to offer their help. It transpired that one of them had a motor service centre in Darwin and offered to give Bridget a compression check the next day. We would have to wait and see if the problem was serious or just something simple.

Bridget's engine was not well. Having arrived in Darwin my first priority was to ascertain how serious Bridget's engine problem was. I called Barry Fowler, the bloke I had met on Sunday, around a hundred miles south of the city.

We arranged for me to take Bridget over around midday to check the engine's compression. On arrival we conducted a vacuum test which, together with the compression test, confirmed that there was a problem with cylinder number three. Either a piston ring was broken or the valves were worn. Either way it would need to wait until Bridget and I returned to Perth. I put an oil additive in the engine that would help reduce any damage and also changed the spark plugs, checked the points and timing.

Meanwhile, the news was that the road from Darwin to Broome was closed to traffic by flood water at Victoria River. The level was three metres above the bridge. It meant that it was likely we would have to stay at Darwin for several more days.

Temperatures in that part of Australia are normally higher than almost all other state capitals but on this particular day a new record was almost set with Darwin actually having the lowest temperatures of them all. At thirty degrees centigrade it wasn't actually cold but there was a low over the area that was expected to deliver more rain. Sydney was the city to spoil the record by staying just one degree lower than Darwin, meanwhile the rest of Australia was sweltering with some of the highest temperatures since 1908! Temperatures in the Gibson Desert of Western Australia reached fifty-five degrees centigrade.

Darwin is a clean, modern and well designed city with plenty of green park areas and community facilities. The city was devastated in 1974 by Cyclone Tracy, giving the local authority the opportunity to rebuild.

Although the area is naturally beautiful, with long warm sunny periods for much of the year and a temptingly cool looking bright blue sea, the attraction of plunging into the surf has to be resisted. In addition to all the usual dangers around the coast up there, the waters are infested with salt water crocodiles and box jelly-fish, both of which can cause human fatalities. A local aquarium has a captured salt water crocodile called 'Bertie'. He is almost seven metres long, more than double the length of Bridget, and weighs in at 690 kilos. Enthusiasts who would like to get a close look at him can enter a perspex container that is lowered into the tank. If it is near to feeding time he becomes quite demented.

I finally left Darwin on the 2nd February even though the Victoria Highway was still closed. I drove Bridget down to Katherine, some two hundred miles south and that much closer to the Victoria River crossing, which meant as soon as the road reopened we could get straight across. Meanwhile I intended to explore the Katherine Gorge.

Bridget's engine hadn't improved and continued to leak petrol from one of the carburettors for much of the time.

The Katherine River is some twenty miles from the town of Katherine and comprises of thirteen gorges. I took a trip in a high speed inflatable craft down the first three gorges whilst the river was still in flood. The craft and passengers get tossed around like the proverbial cork but the scenery makes it worth the effort. After the trip I went for a coffee in the visitor centre and looking down from the veranda into the water I spied a crocodile. It was close to the bank, resting against a tree. Some of the centre rangers came over to confirm the sighting and check that it was a fresh water crocodile and not a 'salty'. The salt water crocs are able to swim up the river during floods and have to be trapped and returned to the estuaries. This was a fresh water breed and about three metres long. The rangers said that unlike salties they rarely bother humans and I just took their word for it. I wasn't at all sure that anyone had told the crocs.

More rain and floods occurred on the Queensland coast and the north-east of the state including Charters Towers. Typhoon Ellie came ashore at Ingham and monsoon rains followed throughout the area causing even more flooding. I was just hoping that the rain wouldn't come over to where we were and cause the Victoria to rise again. The latest report was that the road ahead was still closed to all traffic.

On the evening of 10th February the road condition report said that the flood level at the Victoria River crossing was receding and the water across the road beyond Timber Creek was passable for high clearance vehicles. As long as there was no further rain that evening I resolved to leave the next morning and attempt to get through even though Bridget could not be considered a high clearance vehicle by any stretch of the imagination.

So on the morning of the 11th February I left Katherine and took the Victoria Highway towards Kununurra. I was apprehensive, to put it mildly, largely as a result of many of the anecdotal reports you hear from people who know of others who have been swept off the road by strong currents, or became victims of flash flooding. The actual frequency of such happenings is relatively rare and as long as you employ common sense and approach the water with caution you should be reasonably safe. That's what I kept telling myself anyway, every time I looked at the edge of the tarmac and saw the floodwater lapping there. Really my main concern was my lack of experience of these conditions and what the correct actions would be in any given circumstance, but I thought I'd pick it up along the way.

I mentally broke down the journey into three segments, the first being from Katherine to the Victoria River crossing, then to Timber Creek and finally on to Kununurra. Several of the floodways had water crossing the road but in each case it was little more than three to four inches and hardly moving. When I reached the Victoria River, however, it was in full flood and a frightening sight, but the road was clear so I crossed quickly and carried on to the local roadhouse for a strong coffee. Roadhouses are always good for getting road condition reports because of the constantly passing traffic, although I should say here that in the one hundred and twenty mile drive from Katherine I only saw four other vehicles. Anyway, the chap was able to assure me that there was little water across the road between there and Timber Creek but after that Bridget might not be able to cope.

We continued the fifty miles to Timber Creek and stopped again to refuel and ask about the road. Just as we stopped, a chap in a Mitsubishi car pulled up and asked if I had come via the Victoria River, which I affirmed. He asked the conditions and I told him that it was fine as long as there was no more rain and then I asked about the road from Kununurra. To my delight he said that although there was some water over the floodways I should have no difficulty, and indeed we didn't.

We arrived at Kununurra during a storm and throughout the night there was a violent thunderstorm. The following morning I heard that the Victoria had risen around three metres and the road was again closed. The road ahead was said to be passable through to Fitzroy Crossing but I would need to take special care at Telegraph Hill and Fletchers Crossing.

Given the previously recorded engine troubles that Bridget had, she drove quite superbly from Katherine. We had been cruising at a steady fifty-five to sixty miles per hour and she showed no further inclination to leak petrol from either carburettor. The temperature on the second day was ideal at around a mere twenty-nine degrees but it rained more or less continuously, so at least Bridget did not overheat at all.

I had almost forgotten the warning about the water at Telegraph Hill when we came upon it and I wasn't at all sure that we would be able to get across. I got out of the car, took off my sandals and walked into the water. If there were any salties about they would be no match for my sweaty feet. At its deepest the water was around a foot but with the flow it would build up against the car to around eighteen inches and there were potholes in the road caused I think by the water. At that moment another car came down the road and I told the lady driver the depth. I was brought up always to make way for ladies and this was not going to be an exception. I watched carefully as she drove across and decided that Bridget should be OK. I chose the line of attack carefully and we managed to avoid the potholes. Keeping the engine revs high, Bridget drove through like a veteran.

The second crossing at Fletchers was deeper and the current was faster. I had just decided I might wait for the level to recede a little when a roadtrain came along. He pulled up beside me and, opening the passenger door, leant out and said, "Keep over to the left as far as you can and follow behind me closely. My lorry will break the water for you, but if you get stuck I will pull you out." I recognised the driver as a chap I had spoken with earlier whilst filling up with petrol at Kununurra and I was very grateful for his assistance. It worked perfectly and the remainder of the journey to Halls Creek was mundane but wet.

According to the road report the remaining journey via Fitzroy to Broome was now passable for all vehicles but care was required at floodways where water was across the road. This was great news as I had received several opinions that the road would not be suitable for Bridget today. We left Halls Creek at ten minutes to eight o'clock and had an interesting but uneventful drive to Fitzroy Crossing. The scenery was quite beautiful at times and I had become so accustomed to the fact that water was often lapping at both sides of the road that I was able to more or less ignore it.

However, the swollen Fitzroy River at the crossing was violent and brought me down to earth very effectively. Once again my mind was irrationally concentrating on flooding and what actions I should take if we got marooned by rapidly rising water levels. Then we happened upon some water across the road that was different to anything I had previously seen but had been aware could happen. It was no deeper than previously experienced but it covered a distance of at least a quarter of a mile, much further than we had formerly been exposed too. Bridget took it all in her stride, which was more than could be said for me. However, we got through and then I saw the water just beyond the Willane Bridge Roadhouse and understood what one person had meant, when he had referred to the 'Inland Sea'. It was like a huge lake stretched out on both sides of the road for as far as the eye could see, with an occasional tree sticking out from the water as a reminder that "This should be dry land". It certainly made me very nervous until we were within thirty miles of Broome, after which I settled down.

We arrived safely at around five o'clock in the afternoon and it had stopped raining!

Not unreasonably I felt that the worse was behind me as I had been told by the people in Broome that the road to Port Hedland was not normally subject to flooding. The rain stopped shortly after we left and the temperature started climbing. Bridget was still running well and I looked forward to another good day travelling. The landscape south of Broome is again different to any that I had previously seen in Australia, with miles and miles of what I would call 'savannah'. It put me in mind of what I thought the great American prairies must be like.

After about ninety miles I saw a car at the side of the road and an aboriginal man with it, so I pulled over to see if I could help. The car was an old Nissan that had seen much better days and the chap told me that he thought the battery was flat. I looked under the bonnet and noticed that the battery was brand new, which the chap confirmed. He said he had bought it the day before. The lead to the distributor was not connected so I fixed that and asked him to try to turn the engine over. No electrics worked at all. Realising the problem was far more serious than a flat battery, I offered to try towing him to the next roadhouse, a distance of about one hundred and fifty miles. Bridget struggled for around ten miles and then she started to overheat. We agreed that the chap would stay with the car and I would tell people at the roadhouse that he was there.

Some twenty miles up the road I spied a Toyota Land Cruiser at the side of the road with more aboriginal people so I pulled over and told them about the chap I had tried to help. They said they already knew about him and were going to go there later. After I continued on my way I thought about several inconsistencies in the complete event and realised that the car was almost certainly an abandoned one that the aboriginal was hoping to 'rescue', and the battery had been taken there the previous day in the hope of starting the engine. Just another experience for me.

The rain returned with about one hundred and fifty miles to go and there was more water across the road again. The ground was so wet it only took a little storm to raise the level to critical. We arrived in Port Hedland at around four in the afternoon, after a journey of some four hundred and thirty miles. Bridget handled it so perfectly except for the towing incident that I decided to continue without any rest the next morning.

I awoke to the now familiar sound of heavy rain. Having studied my map I had decided on travelling to Karratha, a mere one hundred and fifty miles. Although there were several spots where water was across the road, generally it wasn't too deep and anyway I had picked up another 'shepherd' to see me safely over the worst areas. The next day was going to be much longer; I was driving to Carnarvon, approximately four hundred and fifty miles south. There is no large community between there and Karratha and so it was unlikely that there would be suitable places to stay other than occasional roadhouses. I hoped that we had at last outrun the flooding but once again that was to prove false. With heavy rain accompanying us we set off early. Fortunately the water across the road only affected the first sixty miles, after which I settled down to enjoying the scenery and keeping a look-out for wildlife on the road.

However, near the Cane River, almost one hundred and eighty miles south of Karratha, we mounted a crest in the road to be confronted with an extended stretch of water sweeping across in front of us. I braked and brought Bridget to a halt a couple of feet from the beginning.

The flow appeared faster than I was happy with, so I got out of the car to take a closer look. My concern increased when I saw, at the other side of the water, a vehicle stopped with its doors open. I could see someone walking about and the thought entered my head that he had only just made it across and was trying to dry out his car.

I decided I would have to walk the floodway before making a decision about driving through it. Just as I was removing my sandals, the other vehicle started up its engine, moved forward and then turned around and started to drive towards me. I studied its wheels, trying to gauge the depth of the water, and decided it should be OK as long as the force wasn't too great. The other vehicle turned out to be another Toyota Land Cruiser, a favourite 'off roader' in Australia, and it hadn't had problems crossing, but was waiting for me. It had overtaken me earlier and realised that I might have problems and offered to clear the way and tow me if anything went wrong. Once again the Australians were looking out for me.

The rain storms were becoming less frequent now, broken up by long spells of warm sunshine. During one of these I noticed, off to the horizon on our right, a gathering of very dark clouds, the shape of which was similar to a huge Victorian building with a domed section in the centre. I pulled Bridget over to the side of the road and watched this storm with fascination. The clouds in the centre were almost black and as it progressed I could clearly see forked lightning dancing from both extremes of the shoulders of the storm. I tried several times to catch the lightning on camera, but them the realisation dawned on me "It's coming this bl**dy way." It was travelling surprisingly quickly and it was only as a result of caning Bridget's engine that we managed to avoid the worst of the rain as it passed behind us.

That, finally, was the last of the flood problems and the remainder of the journey was really pleasant. Again Bridget just kept going, even though the temperature remained in the thirties.

From Carnarvon we drove to Geraldton, this time in brilliant sunshine all the way. This left a fairly leisurely final leg of about two hundred and fifty miles to Perth, although I was having some problems over accommodation. It transpired that there was a major golf tournament over the weekend and all the hotels were booked up. Fortunately I found a very reasonable motel that was not too far out of town.

All that remained now was for me to fix up Bridget's engine and give her a thorough service before putting her back in her container for the trip to Argentina. It had been an exciting five months, during which we had covered over twelve thousand miles. That is five hundred miles more than the first leg from Oxford in the UK, to Chennai in India.

We arrived in Australia in October 2008 with little in the way of expectations except some media generated preconceptions, e.g. all sun, sea and surf. Although I knew some of the distances involved in circumnavigating the continent, it still came as a surprise to find my next destination would sometimes be three days driving away. What I was not in any way prepared for were the extremes experienced in Australia, such as weather, flood levels, bush fires and some of the wildlife.

The country is vast and sparsely populated; the people warm, generous, and what I particularly liked, individualistic, but with exceptional community spirit. I believed it may have many parallels with parts of the United States of America, although I doubted that I would find the Americans quite so generous.

It had been an immensely interesting visit, bringing the distance travelled for the first two legs of this adventure to almost twenty three thousand miles. Names, previously unknown, but now indelibly burnt into my memory are the Nullarbor, the Barkly, the Kimberley, Pilbara and Charters Towers.

We were now approximately at the half way point of our journey and I was getting ready to move on to Argentina, where we would join the Pan American Highway. The journey from Fremantle to Buenos Aires was to take Bridget around nine weeks.

With regards to Bridget's health, it was my belief that the valves or a piston ring on number three piston of her engine was broken. The morning after arriving back in Perth I took Bridget back to the Sports Car Garage owned by Tim Harland. We chatted about the symptoms and agreed a course of action that I should take. I removed the head and we checked the valves; there was nothing to implicate them and so I had to remove the suspect number three piston for inspection. Once out it was immediately confirmed that the ring was broken and so I had to remove the others for checking. Two of the other three pistons were showing signs of disintegrating and so it would be necessary to replace both the pistons and rings. I had been very fortunate to make it back to Perth as the separators between the piston rings were breaking up and on one piston the cap was also disintegrating. I can't help wondering if this was partly the result of the fuel supply running so lean very early on in my journey. On looking back at my comments in the diary page for Iran I found a warning of just such potential problems.

Whilst the engine was stripped down Tim also advised me to replace the big end bearings, which I did, and so it resulted in almost a complete re-build.

It was also necessary to replace a windscreen wiper, carburettor breather hoses, and repair the window winders on both passenger, and drivers, doors. Bridget also had a full service including checks on the timing, carburettor tuning and the points and valve clearances. I replaced the waxoil coating underneath the body shell that was washed off by the Australian Quarantine people. All in all Bridget was in first class shape to tackle the third leg of our adventure: South America.

# LANDSLIDES, LATINOS AND ANDES

*Location: Argentina*
*Timeline: 16th May 2009 – 30th June 2009*

Well, we were back after a nine week enforced rest. During the break I took the opportunity to reschedule the remaining journey and was concerned that, due to the hold-ups in Australia, we were running approximately seven weeks late. Although not particularly working against the clock, the implication of the delay was that if we kept to the original route and timescales we would arrive at the Canadian Rockies in November! Not a good plan, so I had decided to motor on slightly faster than I had intended.

I arrived in Buenos Aires early on the 16th May and was raring to go. However, I couldn't contact the shipping agent as they didn't work on Saturdays, so I had to wait until Monday morning to find out if Bridget had arrived.

The President of the MG Car Club of Argentina, Marco Di Paolo, took me to lunch on Sunday along with two fellow members, Pablo Fernitz and John Ortiz. They were able to give me the lowdown on driving conditions, traffic police behaviour and the best route, not only through Argentina but also Chile and Peru. Once again I received a warning about heavy goods vehicles, but as with Australia, the truck drivers were professional, which was a major plus.

First thing Monday morning I called the shipping agent again and they requested that I go to their offices with my passport and the car's papers. Bridget is in Buenos Aires at least, I thought. When I arrived they asked me to sign a legal warranty that they had, but it was written completely in Spanish. They said it was just routine and was never really used, but to me it clearly had prices/costs in the document. I said if it was rarely used then it was clearly unnecessary and I wasn't prepared to sign it without a copy in English. They then produced a document charging me over $900 US for container storage! Another meeting was arranged for the next day and the whole thing referred back to my agents in Australia. Would I ever see Bridget again?

Refusing to allow these things to get me down I did some more sight seeing and decided to let them worry about it.

It was an interesting sort of day. First of all there was a guard changing ceremony at the memorial to those who fell during the 1982 dispute over the Falkland Islands. I then strolled back to the Paseo de los Granaderos memorial statue in Plaza San Martin. I was sitting on a bench minding my own business when a movement off to the right caught my attention. There was a young man who had dropped to one knee in front of a young lady. He reached up and took her hand and it was immediately obvious that he was proposing and the response was equally obvious. I left them to it for a few minutes and then when they were calming down I walked over and asked if they spoke English. It transpired that they were an American couple and my observations were correct. I congratulated them, wished them luck for their future and then asked them to do it all over again just so that I could capture it on film for the website. Typical old man though, I forgot to ask their names.

Thinking that would be it for the day, I returned to my bench and suddenly realised I could hear music playing away behind me and as I didn't have my Ipod with me it had to be something else! Once again I got up and walked a short distance to find a fifty piece symphony orchestra playing various musical pieces that I assumed were mainly from South American composers as I didn't recognise any. I was told this was a community concert celebrating one of their revolutions. As they have had several I didn't like to ask which in case it was the one ousting the British. Anyway, they were excellent and I stayed to listen for about an hour.

I also discovered the reason for the extended journey time that Bridget had to suffer. Instead of the obvious route across part of the Southern Ocean and then the South Atlantic, someone persuaded the shipping line to take the car all the way up the African coast, no doubt hoping Somali pirates would hijack it, then through the Suez Canal, the Mediterranean and finally across the Atlantic. This was followed by hold-ups in the unloading dock area, problems contacting customs agents and finally, the coup de grâce, a dock strike!

Dock strikes can of course last for just a couple of hours or go on for months (particularly if a British style union is involved). In any case, we would not be beaten although we were now stuck there, eating great food and drinking excellent wine in the sun, until at least the following Thursday. I was now going to pass the weekend relaxing, without having to concern myself with being available for meetings with officials or perched on the edge of my seat, half expecting to get the car back.

When I left the shipping agents that morning they were frantically phoning every auto-insurance agent they could find to try and get me insurance to drive in Argentina. This is not a legal requirement in every country I had visited, but until now, when I had to take out insurance there were normally companies at the border or in the port area. However, in Argentina it was not so easy. There were two main reasons for refusal, the first being that the car was too old (I couldn't tell Bridget, she would have been upset), and the second was that she was not registered in Argentina. However, the agents finally found a company that would cover it and by good fortune the cover was also valid in Chile, so I wouldn't need to do this again in a week's time.

To those residents of Buenos Aires who had started to believe that Bridget the Midget was nothing more than a figment of my imagination I could now say, "I've got her!" After spending all day at the docks and seeing countless pleasant, smiling customs officials, I was finally taken to witness the unlocking of her container at three o'clock in the afternoon on Tuesday 26th May. The day had started slowly and looked doomed when I arrived at the docks to be told that the strike was still going on, but then I was told it would end at midday. My assistant from the customs agent used the time to get some of the paperwork processed so that when the container was opened we would only have to wait for verification (searching the contents, basically) and we would be able to take her.

After the container was opened they asked me to reverse Bridget out so that they could inspect her. That was when I found that whoever placed her in the container had left the ignition on and the battery connected! She was unceremoniously pushed onto the concourse. Shortly after, a rescue vehicle appeared and we connected jump leads to the battery. It took several minutes but to my immense relief she started up. We could now leave… but then I was informed that I couldn't leave the docks area because my insurance was not valid until five o'clock.

We eventually arrived back at my hotel around seven pm and I removed the battery for overnight charging. We would leave Buenos Aires on Thursday morning and head towards Mendoza, which should take a couple of days. This is the wine producing centre of Argentina and I thought we would spend another couple of days checking the produce.

Day one of the third leg and I was really quite pleased. We had left the hotel at around eight o'clock in the morning joining the rush hour traffic, which is always a good initiation into driving in a new country.

I had found that often the most difficult part of the journey was getting on the correct road out of cities. You obviously have to watch the traffic at the same time as trying to spot signs and safely execute manoeuvres, so I was particularly pleased that our exit from Buenos Aires was fairly straight forward. All I had to do was locate Highway 7 and follow it.

The road conditions were generally good and the standard of

driving was reasonable. I had forgotten that I still needed to run-in the engine since its rebuild and so we drove along at between forty-five to fifty miles per hour, so as not to exceed three thousand rpm. We covered four hundred miles in Perth before leaving and so we only had to do this for another six hundred miles. At least travelling at that speed gave me more opportunity to look around at the countryside.

West of Buenos Aires is flat and similar to Norfolk, only much larger. As is to be expected, the number of cattle is very high and the same with sheep. Along the way I quickly started spotting lots of birds that I hadn't seen before, including hundreds of pink flamingos. These, and thousands of other water fowl, were at Laguna La Picasa, between Junin and Rufino.

We were stopped by police checkpoints twice. In both cases, as soon as an officer spotted the car they enthusiastically waved us into a lay-by. In the first case the officer approached and spoke to the passenger seat, then feeling a little foolish came round to my window and demanded something or other. I offered my insurance certificate and licence. He then asked me to get out of the car and I had to follow him to the police office. Here he tried several times to communicate unsuccessfully. Eventually I realised he was referring to a double yellow line that is often seen in the middle of the roads here and he was either accusing me of having crossed it or was telling me not too; I really wasn't sure. A fine of one hundred Argentine Pesos was the penalty but if he was hoping I would cough up he was barking up the wrong tree. I had already been told by the MG guys that there were no 'on the spot' penalties. The second instance the officers just wanted to have a good look at the car and didn't even ask for the papers.

We arrived at a small town called Laboulaye and found a very reasonable hotel. Having covered just over three hundred miles we were about halfway to Mendoza, where I intended to stay for the weekend to tighten down Bridget's cylinder head, check the valve clearances and the timing. She had run well that day but her idle speed was a little high and she was missfiring slightly, when her engine was cold. I wanted to make sure she was running perfectly before attempting to cross the Andes.

Just when I thought the day was over, a television crew turned up at the hotel asking for an interview. Someone had tipped them off that Bridget was there. Then to cap it all, instead of them turning out to be the local channel news people as is usual, it transpired that they produce a local 'Top Gear' programme. At least they brought an interpreter who was really very attractive! She had brought her daughter with her, who wanted to see what all the excitement was about, so I assumed she was married.

Friday 29th May and the dawn was extraordinarily beautiful, but by the time I got my camera from the hotel room and returned outside it was all over. The sun rises and falls very quickly in Argentina. It was the start of a cold damp morning, just like a November day in England. Of course the MG 'air conditioning' cannot be turned off and just added to the misery, but at least the sealant I had put around the windscreen reduced the amount of rain coming in from that direction.

Bridget was running really well now and I had almost to restrain her as the speed gradually crept up whenever my attention was taken by something else. At least when we arrived at Mendoza her 'running-in' would be complete and we would be able to step up the cruising speed a bit.

At the provincial border between Cordoba and Mendoza everyone was checked to make sure that nobody was carrying certain foodstuffs. Suddenly a rather beautiful young lady rushed up to me and held out her arms in welcome and kissed my cheek. Clearly I must have fallen asleep and was dreaming. It transpired that she was a presenter on another Cordoba television programme that was transmitted by two different channels on a Saturday and they were returning from covering another story when they spied Bridget. She was accompanied by a camera man and assistant and so another impromptu interview was held, this time at the side of the road. Once again the programme was basically about cars, oh, and young ladies!

We arrived safely in Mendoza late in the afternoon and I asked the receptionist if there was anywhere that I could work on my car. By a stroke of good luck they had a separate parking facility that would be ideal so the next morning I completed the work on Bridget, ready for the drive over the Andes. Mendoza is a pleasant city, quieter and cleaner than Buenos Aires. The region of Mendoza is of course famous for its wine. My personal preference is for reds, which from this region I found full bodied and very fruity. Many Argentineans seem to have a preference for wine from the Malbec grape.

During the evening I wrote my usual notes for the website and uploaded some photographs. Then I accessed the part of the site that receives blog comments from people who have been on the site, which I always liked to respond to personally if I could. This facility also allows me to reject any unsuitable comments before publication. I was surprised to find a very friendly note from the interpreter who I had met in Laboulaye, saying how she would have liked to have stayed for dinner! My assumption that she was married was wrong, she is in fact divorced. This was the start of an intense exchange of e-mails and something that has to be filed as 'unfinished business'.

Before going to bed I thought I would just sit in the lounge and read a local tourist magazine. There was an advert offering a 'lifetime experience' paragliding. I had long wanted to try this and only a few weeks previously had discussed it with my cousin in France, who just thought it was another crazy idea. I asked the hotel reception to enquire if I could go the next day and they were able to make a reservation on my behalf.

The next day started in complete darkness for me. The hotel had a power break just as I awoke and I had to dress in the dark. So with my pants on my head and my sweatshirt inside out, I went down for breakfast.

After breakfast I went for a run, to try to maintain at least some semblance of fitness.

I was collected from the hotel at two o'clock in the afternoon and we proceeded to pick-up two guys from the USA who were staying just down the road from me. Then we headed off to the north of Mendoza. There we found a range of mountains up to around three thousand feet high. We joined another party of lunatics and headed, in two utility trucks, up one of the mountains. The track was very steep and strewn with boulders. Eventually we arrived at the launch area where our paragliding equipment was laid out.

Yes, at last I had found somewhere that I could try paragliding without having to go through various instruction courses or anything else. This was to be a tandem flight with experienced instructors from a height of two thousand five hundred feet. The flight would last around twenty minutes. The instructor showed me where to hold on, once they had pried my hands away from the flagpole holding the windsock. All I had to do was run across the ground and off the cliff! Simple…and fantastically exhilarating. Where I live in Oxfordshire, we have lots of red kites that soar effortlessly across the skies. To me, paragliding felt just as I imagine those red kites must feel. This was another of my ambitions fulfilled and there are very few other things I can think of that will give me such an adrenaline rush as this.

After a quick check of all Bridget's fluids and filling her with fuel, we left Mendoza a little after half past eight the next morning. The plan for the day was to travel two hundred and fifty miles out of Argentina and into Chile. In between were the Andes Mountains.

I was still feeling fairly high after the previous day's paragliding experience so I thought that there might be a risk that whatever the day brought would be overshadowed. I need not have worried.

I got my first glimpse of the Andes as I drove south from Mendoza on Route 7. We turned west towards Uspallata and the mountain range stretched out before us. In nature my two great loves are mountains and deserts, so the sight of what was to come really thrilled me. Having already experienced, earlier on this journey, the foothills of the Himalayas, and having previously walked in the Alps, the Andes and Rockies were the only two major ranges that I had learnt about at school but hadn't yet seen. Now I was only a matter of a few miles away from the first and I still had a visit to the Rockies later on my schedule.

In recent times somebody said to me mountains are all the same, but I believe, like snowflakes, every one is unique. The highest mountain visible to me was over six thousand nine hundred metres (twenty thousand feet). Then the realisation dawned on me: Bridget had to drive over this lot!

She was running really smoothly and now that the engine was 'run in' I increased the revs a little to between three thousand five hundred and four thousand rpm. All gauges were within their respective limits and the engine sounded good too.

We stopped several times en route just to savour the scenery and take some photos. There was a notable chill in the air, however, as we crept towards the snowline. Eventually we arrived at the border crossing and whilst waiting in the queue I suddenly realised that Bridget was not ticking over very well at all. I quickly switched from being proud of the way she had come all the way up the mountain roads to being very concerned that we may have strained something too much. I decided I would need to lift the bonnet before proceeding further but first I would get through the crossing.

I guess when you cross as many borders as we had on this journey, sooner or later a customs official is going to decide to really inspect things closely. Initially there were lots of problems over paperwork that I really did not fully understand. The Argentineans cleared everything and sent me on to the Chileans, who didn't understand why their Argentinean colleagues had not done something differently. I was on the verge of telling them to do their paperwork and leave the

Argentineans to sort out their own problems but decided not to complicate matters further.

Then a particular customs officer decided he wanted everything removed from the car and thoroughly searched. His colleagues seemed amazed and embarrassed but he insisted. What confused me was that he was Argentinean and only concerned with my exit from the country, so what was he worried about me smuggling out? Anyway, a lady official who was helping me remove everything found the postcards of Bridget that I carried and asked if she could possibly have one for her son. I was delighted and told her she was very welcome. I was then given my opportunity for revenge when the officious customs man asked if he too could have one . I refused with total delight. Childish, but it felt so good.

After all the packing and un-packing of the car I realised that I was breathless and my heart was beating really quite fast. Then it dawned on me that the cause was the thin air at that altitude. I also understood why Bridget's engine was not ticking over so well; it was short of oxygen!

Once we left the customs post, the road down from the peaks was quite staggering. It was really excellent MG driving conditions, around hairpin after hairpin and no crash barriers to be seen.

Approaching the city of Santiago we found ourselves on the circular highway and there were no signs for the city centre. I was fairly sure we had gone too far and so took a turning towards where I thought the centre was and followed the traffic. Eventually, whilst waiting in a queue at traffic lights, a police Land Rover appeared in the lane next to me and I wound down my window and asked for directions to the city. I reasoned that if we were close it should be easy to follow his instructions, if not he would probably show me the way. He indicated for me to follow him and ten minutes later we were there. Helpful chaps.

Santiago is a pleasant enough city, with the usual shopping and historic landmarks. Like Buenos Aires, they also enjoy their demonstrations against just about everything. It is very much part of the culture. However, I had had enough of big cities and so decided to strike out into the country fairly quickly.

We left Santiago at around eight am and followed the route recommended by the hotel, which turned out to be OK but not quite perfect. After a short detour I navigated us in the right direction, more or less!

For the first one hundred miles there were hills and mountains in every direction I looked. It was really beautiful and just as I was becoming accustomed to it we turned a bend and there ahead of us was the Pacific Ocean. The first thing to strike me about it were the rollers coming into the shore. They were between ten to fifteen feet high, although the ocean didn't appear to be generally rough. Further on and there were white caps everywhere across the ocean.

With the Pacific Ocean to the west, to the east I could see the snow capped mountains of the Andes. I knew from studying the map that they eventually converge. When they actually came together, it was going to be interesting to see what happened to the road.

Bridget was generally running well although I had detected a slight misfire over four thousands revs. When we arrived in La Serena, a seaside resort town on the coast of Chile, I noticed a service area that did immediate oil changes and as Bridget needed hers changed I pulled in. They did a competent job but then I noticed that once again she had managed to shed one of her bolts that attach the exhaust pipe to the manifold. The Shell garage was unable to help so I decided to stay in La Serena until I could get it fixed. The following morning I sourced a new nut and bolt and after fitting them ensured that all nuts and bolts were tight.

La Serena is a very pleasant place with a great climate. I was there in the winter and the temperature during the afternoon was around twenty degrees centigrade although overnight it dropped to only just above freezing point. The people were extremely friendly and of course Bridget made lots of new friends.

The ocean there, although calm, creates some fairly impressive waves onto the shore. I shot a short photographic study of it and of the sunset. I also noticed that as the sun goes down hundreds of seabirds congregate on the shoreline, and to my delight flights of pelicans swept across the sea only inches from the water. They reminded me of the Dambusters on the final run in to the Mohne Dam.

We left La Serena at half past eight in the morning and headed north once again, on Route 5. The road was single carriageway but in generally good condition. It snaked inland and very soon we were surrounded by hills and mountains. During the first fifty miles the ocean appeared at sporadic intervals but after that we climbed steadily into the foothills of the Andes as they came closer to the coast.

We were in bright sunlight at one stage but immediately ahead of us the cloud appeared just like a huge white solid wall. Obviously, once we got extremely close one could see a little way into it but visibility was down to around fifty metres. Then it closed in all around us and it became damp and quite chilly.

Bridget continued to perform well with only a hint of misfire when the revs were over four thousand rpm. She pulled well up the hills, and there were plenty of them. There were some excellent MG driving conditions with very tight hairpins that, as we were travelling uphill, we could really lean into. We completed a short trip that day of just over two hundred and fifty miles and we stopped at Caldera. Just two more days to the Peru border, all being well.

The following morning on the road again still heading north, I decided to stop and take a photograph where the mountains meet the sea. As I was crossing the road to gain the best view I looked idly out to sea and suddenly realised I was watching a whale! I don't know what type of whale it was but it was only about fifty metres from the rocky shoreline. Of course, I had the wrong lens on the camera and so I raced back for the telephoto lens. By the time I got back the whale had moved about a quarter of a mile away and was diving; when it surfaced again I didn't have time to focus the camera before it dived once more and so I didn't manage to get any pictures. Nonetheless it fulfilled another of my ambitions, which was to see a whale in its natural habitat.

The rest of the days' travel was through stunning scenery and Bridget behaved well again. The journey through Argentina and Chile was proving to be just another Sunday afternoon drive from the car point of view.

The final leg in Chile was three hundred miles of desert. Most would have found this part of the journey boring but I love wilderness areas and so was quite content. I had not realised that there are considerable desert areas on top of the Andes. Bridget was showing off and continued to run well although once again she had tried to shed her exhaust pipe. Admittedly some parts of the highway were in quite poor condition, rekindling memories of India, but on a much lower scale.

I decided we would stop over for the night at Iquique, on the Chilean coast. It surprised me just how high up in the mountains the desert we had traversed that day was. However, the greatest surprise was turning a corner and finding ourselves on a road approximately fifteen hundred feet above the ocean and an almost sheer drop. Very spectacular, new trousers please!

The next day we would cross the border into Peru and thus start another part of our travels.

The run up to the border was truly breath taking. Much of the time I was driving through flat, single coloured desert. However, from time to time, without any warning Bridget would turn a corner around the crest of a mound and there would be a valley with drops of between fifteen hundred to three thousand feet. Eventually I realised the reason that such a huge change could appear without warning is that whilst driving across the desert the landscape appears flat, so massive valleys are not evident until you are right on the rim. The roads drop all the way to the bottom of the valley, only to climb up the other side. Long stretches of the road had no crash barriers even though the drop was almost vertical. If you lose control of your vehicle, for any reason, there is nothing between you and the long drop.

That day we ran out of petrol and Bridget's jerry can came in useful once again. We stopped on the floor of one of the valleys to fill up the tank. I levered myself from the cockpit of the car and unlashed the fuel can. I then came under ferocious attack from a swarm of midges. I retreated to the inside of the car and covered myself liberally with Bushman's best insect repellent before returning to the refuelling. The midges still attacked me but at least the Bushman's kept the stray dogs away!

Our experience at the Chile/Peru frontier was not unreasonable. The whole process was under two hours and two very helpful Peruvian customs officials saw me on my way. Whilst completing the formalities, I also discovered that car insurance is not a requirement for transit tourists. Bridget performed well again, particularly in the way she attacked the mountain climbs, but she had an exhaust problem and a replacement might be required.

The following day continued in much the same manner as the previous, but we came across a one hundred mile stretch of road where the condition deteriorated considerably. Bridget went through a phase of low oil pressure and high temperature, which I eventually put down to the altitude. It corrected itself and other than that she was running well. Although I had been very impressed with the way she pulled up the mountains, the real test was still to come on the drive from Nazca to Cusco, over the Andes. We would be at heights in excess of nineteen thousand feet.

I found the cause of Bridget's exhaust noise and to an occasional knocking I'd heard. Whilst in Australia, in an attempt to cure the exhaust pipe of constantly coming loose, a bracket was spot welded to the pipe and the gearbox housing. After taking several hefty bangs at various times since then, it had broken loose of the pipe, leaving a hole where the weld had been, and the pipe was knocking on the bracket from time to time. I would try to get a replacement but it would probably not be before arriving in the USA.

A note of warning to anyone thinking of joining the crazy brigade and driving in Peru, take extra care on the tight bends in the mountains. In particular, watch out for lorries; they have a propensity to cut the corners as their speed is often too high. One day I saw two that were off the road and one, a cab and trailer, had actually turned over.

It was now Thursday 11th June and it had been a tiring drive from Camana to Nazca. It was not far, only about two hundred and fifty miles, but the road conditions, in places, were poor. The route was the type that can be great fun when driving an MG, or similar car, snaking around mountainsides with sheer drops into the ocean, but it was hard work because of the lorries that I continually had to evade. They were constantly threatening to crush us against the cliff wall. On top of this, the cliffs were very unstable and the road was strewn with fallen rocks. I started the day with the top down but the danger of being hit by falling rocks was so great along this particular route that I eventually put the top up to give me some protection. That said, the scenery was again astonishing. I would now check Bridget over thoroughly in readiness for the next day's drive across the Andes.

There comes a time when logic demands that we assess our strengths and weaknesses, both in ourselves and, if appropriate, within a team. Now was such a time and my conclusion was 'enough is enough'. I therefore executed what the British call a strategic withdrawal. We are famous for it, whenever we are getting a pasting, that is what we do.

We started out on the road to Cusco, the tourist gateway to Machu Picchu, and everything began well. The road was in excellent condition and I estimated that we would arrive around four o'clock that afternoon. Then we ran into a series of roadworks as we climbed the first three thousand feet. The road surface immediately started reminding me, again, of our days in India. The roadworks were spread over a distance of around two miles but after we had passed all of them the road did not get any better, if anything it got worse. I thought it might be temporary and so we soldiered on at around twenty miles per hour, but after twenty-two miles, things were just not improving. With four hundred miles to go, plus, of course, the return journey on Tuesday, I was forced to conclude that Bridget, although willing, would just not make it.

I turned her around and headed back to Nazca and the hotel. I thought that at least I could garage Bridget there and rent a '4x4' that would be able to cope with the route. However, the nearest car rental company turned out to be in Lima, three hundred miles north. Therefore I decided to do what nobody would ever expect of me and catch a *bus*. It left at eight o'clock in the evening and would take fifteen hours. Oh joy!

So that the day was not totally wasted I thought that I would take a light plane flight to view the line drawings that Nazca is famous for. I use the word famous tentatively, as I have to admit, although I recognised the images from a television programme I didn't realise they were in Nazca. I managed to capture some very acceptable photos of some of the drawings. To show what a philistine I am, I found the drawings OK but was more interested in the type of string that they use to hold various parts of the plane on. I thought I could perhaps borrow some for Bridget's exhaust system. Anyway, it was exciting.

It was 13th June 2009 and I was exhausted, partly due to a nightmare of a bus journey and partly to the altitude of the town of Cusco, where I had arrived. My decision not to push Bridget through the Nazca to Cusco route had been vindicated. I did catch a bus, actually a very modern, ultra smart Marcopolo coach, which took almost nine hours to cover the first two hundred and fifty miles of the route. Even with the size, weight and suspension of the bus, the ride was similar to a cruise ship, in a force ten gale, crossing Biscay. I am convinced Bridget would not have made it to and from, Cusco, had we persisted. I was told subsequently that this road was normally quite good but that it had been badly damaged by exceptionally heavy flooding during the previous winter.

It was a great shame because the last two hundred miles were generally as good as the Pan American Highway had been and Bridget would have been made to feel so at home in Cusco. It is a pretty town of around four hundred thousand inhabitants, lots of history, plenty of colour and some pleasing architecture. However, the altitude did take a little getting used too. It affects people differently and I found I was both breathless and my chest felt constantly strained. The locals take lots of cocoa extract, typically around half a kilo each per day, usually either chewed or in tea, and that helps considerably. I should think after that they're beyond caring.

The mountains in this part of the Andes are completely different to the west coast side in that they are covered in vegetation and considerable areas are cultivated. Given that some fields can be as high as eighteen thousand feet and can be on a slope in excess of sixty degrees, everything must be done by manual labour, unless they could find out how to harness goats.

To get to Machu Picchu from Cusco I took a train ride of around three hours. It was fascinating to see the lifestyle of the farming community and the small towns and villages en route. The standard of living appeared far better than I had imagined and the Peruvians do seem adept at taking some of the more desirable items of modern society but retaining many of their traditions. The scenery became increasingly awe-inspiring the closer to Machu Picchu the train got and the mountains started taking on the shape and appearance of that normally associated with this location; almost steeple shaped and covered in lush vegetation. Then the first of the Inca ruins came into view as the train pulled to a halt.

For those who aren't familiar with the history of Machu Picchu, the name is in fact that of the mountain; the name of the Inca city was lost in the depths of time. I was told by a guide that the name means 'whole mountain'. The Inca period was far more recent than I thought, scanning from fourteen hundred to fifteen hundred AD. Nobody knows why, but the inhabitants abandoned the settlement just before the Spanish Conquistadors arrived and the jungle reclaimed it so that, other than for some local farmers, it became a 'lost city'. It was rediscovered by Hiram Bingham in July 1911, whilst searching for a completely different Inca city.

Back in Cusco that evening, I was to return on the nightmare bus service to Nazca to be reunited with Bridget and get back on the road. In the meantime, I walked into the main square where there were crowds gathering; lots of locals in traditional costumes and countless groups of children, all dancing to the beat of drums and Indian pipes. Evidently it was a rehearsal for the Inti Raymi or Sands Party, sometimes also referred to as the Festival of Sun. I have since established that this is the second largest festival in South America. Hundreds of thousands of people converge on Cusco from other parts of the nation, South America and the world for a week long celebration marking the beginning of a new year. The centerpiece of the festival is the all-day celebrations on June 24, the actual day of Inti Raymi. On this day, the ceremonial events begin with an invocation by the Sapa Inca in the Koricancha square in front of the Santo Domingo church, built over the ancient Temple of the Sun. Here, the Sapa Inca calls on the blessings from the sun. Following the oration, Sapa Inca is carried on a golden throne, in a procession to the ancient fortress of Sacsayhuamán, in the hills above Cusco. With the Sapa Inca come the high priests, garbed in ceremonial robes, then officials of the court, nobles and others, all elaborately costumed according to their rank, with silver and gold ornaments.

I returned to Nazca from Cusco by the same means that I had gone there, bus, and the second trip was no better than the first. I was pleased to see Bridget again and gave her a wash, then took her into town and found a garage that would weld repair her exhaust. That done, I was ready to get back on the road towards Ecuador.

Driving had become so much less stressful now that Bridget was running properly. I decided not to visit Lima as I had had enough of major cities for now, particularly capitals, which are not at all representative of the country as a whole. The Pan American Highway seemed, if anything, to be getting even better. The scenery continued to be interesting, although it was changing from the southern half of the country and must be more fertile as commercial agriculture was very evident here.

As I got nearer to Lima, the traffic got worse. Congestion had rarely been a problem in South America compared to Europe, or Asia for that matter. On this day, however, I noticed a number of similarities to India. Firstly, the amount of traffic, then there were the driving standards and the free-for-all tactics used at congested junctions. Also the reason for the congestion at junctions was the accumulation of buses and all types of taxis dropping off and/or picking up passengers. In a bay designed for two vehicles, there would be anything up to a dozen and if that meant stopping and blocking three of the four traffic lanes, then so be it. This resulted in the moving traffic, and I use the term loosely, trying to funnel into a single lane with the resulting chaos and bad temper seen throughout India.

As we neared Lima, cruising down a relatively clear road, a lorry and trailer pulled out from the side where, I eventually realised, he had been waiting for his chum in an identical HGV. I pulled into the outside lane to avoid the first truck, only to be confronted by his chum pulling out of a junction on the left into the outside lane and boxing me back in behind the first HGV. The second HGV then decided to pull behind his mate, ignoring completely that that was where Bridget and I currently were. There were times when an anti-tank gun on a mounting in the passenger seat appeared a good idea.

The Pan American Highway actually takes you more or less through the centre of Lima and here the traffic was extremely heavy. I positioned myself in the centre lane whenever I could, to make it as easy as possible to move left or right. Undertaking, as well as overtaking, is quite normal in South America, and so I had vehicles moving and jostling on both sides of Bridget. We were just entering an underpass when suddenly a wheel careered out from underneath a taxi and crossed the road immediately in front of me. I was watching the wheel and trying to decide where it would go and at what speed I would need to drive to avoid it, without swerving into the path of another vehicle. I was also trying to anticipate what other drivers would do when they noticed it. Anyway, I managed to avoid hitting it or anybody else and as far as I could see it did not cause an accident.

During the day I had to stop twice for fuel, eight times for toll booths (the first I had seen in Peru) and six times at police checkpoints. The final checkpoint was manned by no less than a dozen officers. The one who waved me down shouted to his colleagues and approached the window to speak to me. I knew from experience exactly what he would want but I always pretended to be puzzled. He greeted me in Spanish and I returned the salutation in English. I had learnt never to use anything but English where officials were involved. He eventually made it clear he wanted to see my documents, which I retrieved from my briefcase. Then he wanted something else but it genuinely wasn't clear what it was. I checked that I had given him all the usual things. Then he removed his wallet and showed me his driving licence. This was the first time I had been asked for my British licence after I had presented my international one. He was now happy, but a shout went up from one of his colleagues who clearly was not happy. He came over to join us and waved a small book under my nose, pointing to a particular item. I put my glasses on and peered at his book, but it was all in Spanish.

Once more I said, "I don't understand Spanish, only English." Then he started tapping on the steering wheel through the open window and was saying something else in Spanish in the hope I would understand that. When I didn't, he repeated it twice more so that I would understand. Impasse. Whilst he thought about how to approach the problem differently, I had time to re-collect something that I was told only the previous day: it is technically illegal to drive any right-hand drive vehicle in Peru. However, the border officials still allow such vehicles into the country. It appears that this is a relatively recent law and was introduced to combat a scam involving the importation from Japan of cheap, second-hand, right hand drive cars of dubious roadworthiness.

Meanwhile, the officer took out a notebook and proceeded to draw the inside of my car with the steering wheel on the left. This he thrust under my nose, so I took it and said, "No, no, no, it's here, look," and crossed out the steering wheel and drew it on the right. The officer was apoplectic. I thought for one moment he was going to have a heart attack or at least burst a blood vessel. He clearly concluded that I must be one of those inbred Englishmen incapable of comprehending even basic Spanish. With ill hidden feelings of frustration he suggested I go. Suddenly I understood and said, "Thank you, goodbye." This was not the first time that I had found it helpful to deny any understanding of what was being said. People usually give up in frustration and allow you to continue doing whatever it was you wanted to do in the first place.

Thursday 18th June and the weather in northern Peru was overcast, with occasional light rain. It had been another day of beautiful but changing scenery; glimpses of the coast, at times spectacular, interspersed with desert and multi-coloured mountains. I have never seen mountains quite the same as the ones that day. The colours ranged from a rich brown to pale yellow and a peculiar sort of olive green in some areas. At times, some of the mountains looked almost like a patchwork quilt.

It appeared that the further north we went, the worse the driving standards became. There were several occasions when I was faced with an oncoming HGV in my lane and had to take avoiding action. The condition of the road surface started poorly but once north of Chimbote it was brand new and excellent, and for a second time I had a police officer trying to explain that Bridget was illegal!

We reached Trujillo and I had started to try and contact shipping agents to arrange the sea trip from Guayaquil in Ecuador to Panama. All things being equal, we should cross the Desierto de Sechura to Sullana the next day, which would put us right by the Ecuadorian border.

We made Sullana without trouble. My only concern was that every garage around had only eighty-four and eighty-nine Octane fuel and we needed to fill up very soon. I only hoped that if we filled up with that, it wouldn't cause Bridget's engine any upset.

The final part of the journey to the frontier was fairly straightforward, I suppose. I was a little uneasy about it for some reason, nothing I could pinpoint but a number of small things didn't seem quite right. The road to the border was fairly poor compared to the usual Pan American Highway, and at the crossing point it appeared to be all locals travelling backwards and forwards. There were no international travellers and almost no heavy goods vehicles, which you normally get at a crossing. Also, the customs and border guards seemed unsure of how to treat me.

There was a small problem over the paperwork, leaving Peru. At first the formalities went smoothly, with the head customs officer entering my details and Bridget's into his computer. The program found our entry details that had been completed when we arrived, but then a puzzled look crossed the official's face. He looked at me and said, "Toyota?" and pointed towards Bridget. "No," I replied, "MG." This started a hiatus that would take the best part of an hour to resolve. It transpired that when we entered the country and the immigration officer was entering our details, his computer program offered a list of car manufacturers that did not include MG, but he had to enter something before the program would allow him to continue. Not unreasonably, he chose a manufacturer at random which turned out to be Toyota, but, here I was with what to this border official appeared to be a different car!

We eventually unravelled what had happened and they allowed me to continue across the frontier. However, even though this was the main border crossing between Peru and Ecuador, it is rare for foreigners to cross here with cars and the Ecuadorian authorities seemed equally unsure of what paperwork should be done, but eventually let me in.

I had received a couple of warnings about a different type of hazard that can confront you in this country, that of landslides. I was hoping that the landslide 'season' had finished. There is a warning on the UK Government website about this problem so we would need to keep an eye out.

It was now the 23rd June 2009 and precisely one year since Bridget and I left the UK on this adventure. When we started I had no idea of the challenges and experiences ahead of us or even if we would get much beyond Germany, but here we were almost finishing the South American leg.

I had been fortunate enough to meet hundreds of beautiful people and made some marvellous new friends. My thoughts at this time were also very much with those people that I had met in Iran and Pakistan. Iran had held elections and the outcome was challenged by some as fraudulent. This sparked street demonstrations causing brutal retaliation from government troops and police. I was concerned for the safety of the many friends I had made there. Also, the security situation in Pakistan was worsening and again I feared for the safety of those that had been so helpful to me.

We had crossed the border into Ecuador with me feeling uneasy about the route I had chosen. I should have researched the Pan American more deeply but having looked at the map I believed that the route I had chosen was the Pan American. However, the condition of the road did not comply with any description I had ever seen of the Pan American Highway.

Bridget had just undertaken the toughest challenge she had faced so far. The road surface no longer existed on much of the route, but I checked my maps and this really was the Pan American Highway. The conditions were as bad as those between Cusco and Nazca, when I had refused to take Bridget further. In this instance I had little choice short of returning to Peru and trying another route, but in Australia I established the policy of not going back just because it was tough.

The road climbed thousands of feet and then plunged down the other side, which was causing Bridget a problem given the poor fuel quality of eighty-nine octane. The road surface was often non-existent. Potholes were large, deep, and frequent. It reminded me of the journey from Goa to Mangalore but to make it really exciting Ecuador also offered us landslides.

In the UK, if a few cubic feet of mud slides onto a railway line and causes the eight fifteen am train from London to Brighton to be late, it makes headline news. In Ecuador, when they refer to a landslide they are talking about a large slice of the side of a mountain. There are thousands of cubic feet of mud moving down the side of the mountain either blocking or removing large sections of road and sometimes burying complete communities. More than once I rounded a bend to find a fork created in the road because of a landslide; one way took you down the old road which was blocked and the other took you down the new route. There were no signs to suggest which you should take. If this was not enough there were many rocks, and I don't mean stones, that had rolled down the slopes and were just waiting for a low clearance vehicle to come along.

If the roads were clear and the mountains more stable, this would make excellent sports car driving. Unfortunately it was too dangerous to stop and take any photographs because the chances were that a bus or truck would round a bend and hit Bridget. If only the video camera had been working, I could have captured some rare footage, but I dropped it when paragliding in Argentina and it hadn't worked since. On the occasions that I was able to look away from the road, the spectacle was fantastic. Clearly we were in the centre of the Ecuadorian Andes and it was just beautiful, but don't let it hold your gaze or you will regret it. If a pothole doesn't break a stub axle then a rock will fracture a shock absorber. The conditions eased after approximately eighty miles and we arrived safely at Catamayo for our first night in Ecuador. I had decided that Bridget deserved a day's rest and a little pampering after such a bone shaking day. Her engine temperature was in the red sector more than once, but at least I had now filled her up with what I was told was ninety-five octane petrol.

The town of Catamayo is small, a little dusty but with some reasonable restaurants and hotels. The hotel I stayed at was mainly staffed by young ladies, one of whom was very attentive. Although she was only twenty-five years old, the culture in that part of the world has a different take on relationships with 'older' people. It was a very pleasant interlude on my journey.

From Catamayo we had a simple drive to Cuenca, only a matter of around two hundred miles. The first twenty-five miles were very good. The road surface was smooth and although we still had to tackle the mountain gradients, Bridget seemed fine.

Somehow I missed a vital junction at the town of Loja without immediately realising it. I kept seeing and following signs for Cuenca so thought all was well although the road surface was now deteriorating somewhat. We came to a section that was no more than a farm track but that was not unusual. However, after a couple of miles of this I began to suspect the worse. Unfortunately people kept confirming that we were on the road to Cuenca. Indeed, even though it appeared to be a farm track, there were still road signs all along it. After we had travelled around twenty miles on this road, a few checks with the map confirmed that although we were indeed heading to our destination, we were certainly not on the Pan American Highway any longer. The question was, should we return to Loja and find the correct road or press on? We pressed on until, rounding a corner, I saw a bus parked at the side of the road and the driver waving frantically at me to stop. A landslide had totally blocked the road and it was unlikely to reopen that day. He told me that there was an alternative road over the mountain that meant I would not have to go all the way back to Loja. He also confirmed that Bridget should be OK.

We found the road only two miles back and although a little doubtful, we set off. Two things were immediately evident: first, if we met something coming the other way there was no possibility of passing, and secondly, there was no way we could turn around and go back. We met two senior ladies walking towards us and they confirmed that this road would take us to Cuenca and it was passable, but one of them was gesturing and trying to tell me that either something was as deep as her thigh or that she needed a hip replacement! I wasn't at all sure about this anymore but we were committed.

It soon became evident what the lady was warning me of. Rain water falling on the mountains runs down and across the track carving deep clefts and leaving a deep quagmire. Some of these were indeed very deep and had steep banks in and out. It was only the extra weight in, and on, Bridget's boot that enabled us to get through these by giving extra traction, but features such as the exhaust pipe prevented us reversing down the mountain. Then there were a couple of sections were erosion had reduced the width of the track to only a little more than Bridget's width and there were large fissures where the track was breaking away from the mountain. With a drop I dared not more than glance at, we sped through these chicanes as our weight may have been all that was needed to start more slides.

We eventually met up with a wider, smoother track, which took us into a small town called Santiago. We stopped whilst I got out to ask a lady for directions. On getting back in and closing the door there was a dull thump. I looked around and the driver's wing mirror had dropped off. I was embarrassed as she was calling out to everyone to come and see this car. I had a small crowd of people all watching as I tried to refit the mirror with some gaffer tape supplied by one of the residents. We rejoined the Pan American Highway a couple of miles up the road. I kept saying, "It's all experience," and that day it certainly was.

Santa Ana de los Ríos de Cuenca, to give it its full title, is a very pleasant city and home to another World Heritage site. The city's Cathedral de la Inmaculada and Plaza Abdon Calderon were designated heritage site status in the year 2000. The architecture throughout the city centre I found very interesting and they have so many churches that they must be very good people. I can confirm they are certainly very friendly, anyway.

My last days in Ecuador were spent in Guayaquil. This is Ecuador's largest port and an intriguing city in that nothing is what it appears to be. The cathedral, at first glance, is a magnificent structure, probably from the eighteenth or early nineteenth century. In fact, when you look closer at the detail you will notice that the beautiful stained glass windows are actually modern, what I would refer to as printed. As late as 1915 the building was little more than a large brick-built warehouse with a reasonably imposing frontage. There is also a clock tower which would not look out of place on the esplanade of an English seaside resort; indeed the clock was purchased from England in 1842 and is still keeping good time. They could teach the Swiss a thing or two about timepieces. Although I am guessing I would say there are very few, if any, buildings there that are a hundred years old and in their original appearance. That does not detract from the fact that it is a pleasant city with a number of attractions. However, this area's main attraction for tourists has to be that it is the jump-off point to the Galapagos Islands.

Unfortunately I had neither the time nor money to spend on visiting them and so I did the next best thing, which was to cross the road from my hotel to Seminario Park. Here there is a large colony of iguanas, turtles and Ecuadorian squirrels. For some reason I had never considered iguanas as tree climbers because their size and demeanour doesn't suggest it likely, but they actually spend much of their time doing just that. The larger ones are several feet long and their girth must be up to eighteen inches. When walking through the park, if you look up, and be very careful how you do that with such large beasts above you, you can see them resting on branches much smaller than the iguana's girth.

I had been a little pre-occupied trying, in vain, to get Bridget loaded into a container for the trip to Panama. The ship was due to leave on Tuesday 30$^{th}$ June and this was Saturday 27$^{th}$ June. I returned to my hotel having spent over five hours trying to gain access to the port only to be refused entry because a particular piece of paper was missing and the chief honcho was not working today, so nobody would complete the process. We had to return Monday morning to make a final attempt or miss the boat. My only consolation was that a very attractive young lady, called Karlita, was acting as interpreter, which meant spending a lot of time in her company! I wondered, if I missed the boat would she show me around?

Monday came and success at last. The paperwork was accepted and I drove Bridget into the port area. There I met the main contender for 'most officious customs officer in the world'. We locked horns very early in the proceedings and things went downhill from there. At one stage he indicated that he wanted the engine removed at which point I said, "If you want the bloody thing out you can f***ing well do it yourself, sunshine." After such an inexcusable outburst he appeared to become more reasonable, but everything was removed from the interior and the boot. However, after all the games Bridget finally was put to bed in her container. She had become such a beast since her engine rebuild that they tied her down in much the same way as the safari guys secure big game when transporting them; each wheel was lashed with ropes tied off at an angle of around one hundred and ten degrees. I returned to my hotel to organise a flight for myself and have a farewell dinner with Karlita.

My journey through South America had been memorable for many different reasons. First, and foremost, was the scenery throughout almost the total route; the desert areas and of course the Andes, sometimes completely barren and at others covered in dense vegetation. Secondly were the children, so clearly the core of many indigenous communities throughout the South American countries. Then the driving; probably some of the most punishing for Bridget, but also the most exhilarating for me once we had completed each section. The drive over the mountains to Cuenca will always be with me. Finally, of course, the ladies. God bless them.

My last night in Guayaquil was exceptionally poignant and will stay with me forever. My shipping agent's partner makes a considerable contribution to local charities. She asked if I would like to visit one of the projects that she was managing and jointly funding with the Ecuadorian Government. The whole area was, until two years earlier, waterlogged swamp which had now been reclaimed and given over to a large population of the city's poorest residents. They were building a school, which I was shown around, that by European standards would be considered basic but for them was palatial, and in addition there were several community projects being piloted. The most ambitious was a self-help employment scheme that they hoped would eventually provide work to one hundred individuals. The plight of the children in the shanty buildings was difficult to comprehend but they displayed amazing resilience and, above all, hope.

Bridget and I would be back in action around the 8$^{th}$ July, when we would tackle Central America.

# THE EARTH MOVED FOR ME

*Location: Panama to Mexico*
*Timeline: 3rd July 2009 – 24th July 2009*

It's a funny old life, sometimes it would be better to just go back to bed and wait for tomorrow. My first day in Panama and I came down to breakfast early; I had to as the traffic noise outside my bedroom window made it impossible to sleep any longer. The hotel agreed to move me into a quieter room and I should have realised then that it would be best to stay there.

Breakfast was normally a very straightforward affair; cereal, fruit juice, toast and marmalade and coffee. Toast; the most common breakfast item anywhere in the world, except Panama. They have a kitchen where the chef will prepare all sorts of delicious dishes from around the globe, but he can't do toast!

I took a taxi to the shipping agent, my first priority, so that any paperwork problems could be sorted out before Bridget arrived on the Monday. The agent wanted money before he would do anything. I explained that all costs had been paid to the agent in Ecuador, but he looked doubtful and I had a funny feeling that this subject was going to come back again on Monday.

When I had finished at the agents I discovered that my mobile phone didn't work in Panama and so I decided to go to the shops and perhaps buy another one that would work in every country from there to Canada. This I managed and then thought I should get some more cash from an ATM. I tried four and they all said that they couldn't complete the transaction and referred me to my bank. Perhaps the global financial crisis had at last caught up with me and I made a mental note to check my e-mails that evening to see if there was one from my financial advisor saying, "Come home Roy, you're broke."

With only $20 in my pocket I decided that I would have to change some traveller's cheques for my immediate needs. None of the eight banks I tried would change the cheques, including such international institutions as HSBC, BNP and Citibank. As they all sell this product in most European countries, they should be prepared to accept them at any of their branches.

Then to finish off the day, as I started out at a brisk walk for the hotel, the skies literally opened and one of the noisiest thunder storms I have witnessed in a very long time emptied itself all over me. Somebody said it wasn't personal, but I was not so sure. Perhaps the next day would bring a ray of sunshine, it couldn't get much worse; could it?

It was five minutes to two o'clock in the morning and I was awakened by the whole room shaking violently. It was as if this concrete and brick structure was in fact made from jelly and someone was shaking the plate it stood on. Panama had just suffered an earthquake. Even though I had never experienced such an event before I found I was getting out of bed even as I awoke, but my brain was questioning what was going through my mind.

I jumped into a pair of shorts, left my room and immediately the situation was confirmed. People were milling about and it became clear that as a heavy sleeper I was one of the last to wake. I walked from my fifth floor room down to the hotel lobby and most people were making their way outside. A night porter told me that such a strong quake was very unusual and that we should wait in case of aftershocks. We wouldn't know until the morning what strength the quake was or if we were only on the periphery of it. I was amazed that the hotel had no evacuation procedures for such events, even if they are rare, as Panama is on a major geographical fault line.

News reports confirmed that the earthquake was centred on the

Panama/Costa Rica border, some four hundred miles north of Panama City. It measured six point two on the Richter scale and was at a depth of fifteen miles. Initial reports said that there were no reported casualties or damage although subsequently it was reported that some buildings collapsed near the border and three of the luxury multi-story buildings in Panama City had developed large cracks.

Sunday evening 5th July we had another quake, this time measuring only five point three on the Richter scale, so it hardly counted!

Although still a few miles away, I was also keeping an eye on the situation in Honduras where the elected President was removed in a coup and, having been forcibly exiled, was threatening to return to his country. There had been some street protests and riots from his supporters but I was hoping it would be peacefully resolved before I got there. Personally I was backing the 'BRIDGET for PRESIDENT' campaign, although she would have to fulfil several overseas visits before getting down to sorting out the domestic issues.

Friday 10th July, I went with the local agent to Colon which is the port where Bridget was delivered. We presented a dozen copies of various documents to the authorities the previous day and they confidently said that I would be able to collect the car that day. We duly reported to the main port customs office just after eight o'clock and were greeted by a gentleman who seemed to know my agent. We then waited for the statutory minimum of three and a half hours for the chief honcho before being told he was not coming to the office after all and so the man we first met signed our papers and stamped them with considerable official flair. From there we went to the container port where they would bring the container to us to be opened in the presence of a customs officer.

Forty-five minutes later, the container arrived. I checked the numbers on the seals to be sure they hadn't been changed and the customs officer watched as the doors were opened. He then went back to his office and left us to undo all the ropes, etc., that had held Bridget in place for the journey. Things were going well and all the papers were stamped, copied and signed. The last thing remaining was for the customs officer to check the car and contents and we could be on our way. He came out, looked around the car smiled and said, "Nice car," and we trooped back into his office. He picked up all the papers and said "NO." They declared her '*Persona non grata*'!

A long exchange of viewpoints then pursued between the agent and the customs officer and it became clear to me that they were discussing the right-hand drive aspect of Bridget. It transpires that Panama have introduced a new law making the driving of such vehicles illegal, just like Peru and for the same reason. They brought in a translator and said I would have to transport the car out of the country; I refused. They said that I should call the British Embassy and I told them the embassy would say "That is your problem." Then one of the officers suggested, absolutely seriously, "Just leave it here and go without it." Yes, I refused, and informed them that we would just stay there until they found a way around the problem. After all, in three days Bridget and I would be in Costa Rica.

Eventually, after many phone calls it was suggested that we go to the local transit office in the town to see if they could help. This we did and the transit office official immediately said that I could have a temporary import licence because I was a tourist and the car is a classic. It would appear that the customs officers are not fully aware of what is and is not allowed, but once again stonewalling paid off. Several new forms had to be completed and then a man sprayed Bridget with some sort of insecticide; the indignity. We were then set free!

Saturday 12th July and I gave Bridget her first six thousand mile service since rebuilding her engine. I am glad to report she was running really smoothly and everything appeared to be in good order. Her rear tyres were starting to wear and I would need to keep an eye on them, but they had been really excellent covering over forty thousand miles since they were fitted.

I was going to get on the road to David, a city in the north of the country near to the Costa Rican border, but then I was told that there was a classic car event in the city the following day so I decided to stay on and leave on Monday. I went along to the event, in the heart of Panama City, in the morning, with no expectation of what I was going to see. It transpired that there are two active, thriving clubs in the country, one for any classic or sports car and the other specifically for American classic cars. Both were represented and there was an interesting turnout of cars including a 1930 and a 1934 Chevrolet as well as a Packard, some Corvettes, a Cadillac and a Stingray. There was also a beautiful Fiat and Alpha Spyder representing Europe, along with Bridget, of course. We were made very welcome, which is the Panamanian way.

Well that was it from Panama City and the following day we would hit the road north towards Costa Rica to see what that held in store for us.

The drive from Panama City to David in the north started well enough. We left at eight o'clock and quickly found the Pan American Highway. Traffic was fairly light and the weather was bright, then becoming hot and humid as the day wore on.

The road surface was not perfect but the potholes were generally avoidable. I relaxed and started to enjoy motoring again. David is a city some thirty miles from the frontier with Costa Rica and approximately three hundred miles from Panama City, so the driving time would not be too long. We were stopped a couple of times at police checkpoints, where the officers were friendly and thought that Bridget was great.

When we were about forty-five miles from David we were following a three tonne delivery truck and on rounding a bend I saw more police. We were almost parallel with them before one of the officers saw Bridget and waved his arm at us and blew on his whistle. We pulled over to the side of the road as quickly as we could but because he was so late in seeing us we were clearly forty yards past him. I reversed Bridget back up to where the patrol car was parked and the officer came over and asked me for my passport and driver's licence. I gave him these and got out of the car. It was quickly obvious that this was no ordinary checkpoint, but a speed check set-up. The second officer was writing and talking to an American male who was later joined by his oriental travelling companion. The American passed some dollars to the officer who took them and tucked them into his ticket book. I was about to say to the American, "There are no on-the-spot-fines in Panama" when I realised this was not a fine! The American said, "No receipt eh, well no record then, fine." With this he left.

On the roof of the patrol car was a hand-held speed gun and whenever a car came towards the checkpoint the officer would look up from his writing and squeeze the trigger, then instruct his partner to pull the car over. The gun was pointed at traffic coming from the opposite direction from which I had arrived. The way in which he was using the gun was totally against the manufacturers operating instructions and in the UK would have rendered each ticket invalid if challenged.

Then the officer said to me that I had been travelling at ninety-two kilometres per hour and the speed limit was sixty to seventy-five kilometres per hour. I said, "Is it sixty or seventy-five, it can't be both?" I added, "The speed gun is on the roof of your car and you were processing the American when I arrived so how do you know what speed I was travelling?" He said that his fellow officer saw me and that is what he said my speed was. I said that if he was that good, why bother buying a speed gun? He said that I would be fined $66 US and waited, clearly expecting me to make an alternate offer. I told him to write out the ticket. He did this and told me to sign the form, which I refused as it was in Spanish and I couldn't read it. He said that I was not to try to leave the country until the fine was paid, and I was somewhat impolite about what he could do with his speed gun.

The following morning we made our way to the border and took just under two hours to get through the formalities, which was really quite good. We entered Costa Rica just after a quarter past ten, having purchased car insurance for this country. In Panama it appears to be optional, but for Costa Rica it is a requirement and can be purchased for $15 US at the frontier.

We started a new navigation system. I tried to purchase a road map of Central America whilst in Panama but couldn't get one anywhere, so I thought we would just use a compass from here on. How difficult can it be to find a complete country!

The drive from the frontier to San Jose, the capital city of Costa Rica, was the most enjoyable, relaxing drive since the Gold Coast in Australia. The road condition was generally good and the scenery was beautiful. Although only just over two hundred and twenty miles from the frontier to the city, the drive does take around four and a half hours, largely because it is single carriageway and a very winding road. There is also a mountain range involved that is beautiful, though not as breathtaking as the Andes. It still rises twelve thousand feet, however, that is around two and a quarter miles high. Bridget went up there like the proverbial rat up a drainpipe. She was showing off and I could only hope that this wasn't the pride before the fall, but I was really pleased with her performance.

San Jose is an expensive city and for the life of me I couldn't figure out why. Prices were similar to many European capitals but there was no other comparison. Fuel prices are sixty percent higher than Panama, hotel rooms were on par with Brussels, Vienna and Florence. Restaurants and bars were much the same as the UK in price terms but far lower quality. Funnily enough though, according to one international report Costa Ricans are the second happiest people in the world! That is qualified as 'happy with their cultural conditions and their government'.

We rested over Wednesday and then struck out on Thursday for Nicaragua. The road condition was once again really very good but it was only a single carriageway and quite winding, so the traffic was bad and progress slow for the first ninety miles. After that, getting to the frontier was a very pleasant experience, with beautiful scenery including lots of mountains again. There are also several volcanoes along the route including some that are currently active. Unfortunately, due to the traffic, the lack of anywhere to park and considerable low cloud, I was unable to take any photos at all in Costa Rica. That was the first country that had happened.

The border crossing was dreadful, taking four hours in all. So it was four o'clock in the afternoon by the time I got back on the road, still with one hundred miles to go. Luckily I made it to Managua as darkness fell, because I had again been warned not to drive here after dark. Nicaragua is one of the poorest countries in Central America, something which is quickly evident. The country itself is pleasant enough, with varied countryside, all very green. Just a couple of miles in from the border there is a huge lake with two classic shaped volcanoes on the far side. Had conditions been better it would have made a great photo but the clouds were black and dusk was falling.

That week had been a serious driving week and the next day I intended to leave Nicaragua, cross Honduras and make for San Salvador, capital of El Salvador. I was going to try and reach the Mexican border over the coming weekend.

Friday's drive from Nicaragua to San Salvador was marred by another awful border crossing from Honduras into El Salvador. The crossing from Nicaragua into Honduras took a little over an hour, which because of the political situation I had thought might take longer, but the crossing from Honduras into El Salvador took nearly five hours and meant driving in the dark to San Salvador, the capital.

With dusk closing in I became aware of the driver of a brown coloured Volvo 760 trying to attract my attention. He was a big chap with a spotted red bandana and blue shirt. He wound down the window of his car and shouted, "How far have you come?" Clearly an American, I thought it best that we stop to have this conversation, so pulled over to the side of the road. He was indeed an American, and an author to boot, with a Costa Rican 'travelling companion'. He said, "I knew you were either a Limey or an Aussie. You are the only ones crazy enough to do it." I took that as a compliment and then he told me he intended to follow me all the way to the States! After all, he reasoned, we would be safer as a pair in Mexico as we could watch each other's backs. I was not at all sure if that made me feel more comfortable or not.

Saturday and as planned Bridget and I moved on to Guatemala City, one day away from the Mexican border. Whilst I was waiting for Bridget in Buenos Aires, I had checked the British government's travel website offering advice on different countries. The advice proffered with regards to Mexico, was to avoid all travel there because of the high level of risk from the swine flu pandemic. They totally ignored any mention of the six thousand murders that took place in the country during the previous twelve months! How can government bodies get such distorted priorities?

Almost everyone kept telling me that Mexico was dangerous, so it was refreshing to get another opinion from an acquaintance that the whole danger 'thing' is over hyped. Certainly crime is a major social problem but so it is in many European countries too, and in the USA. However, tourists are rarely targeted and it's my experience that myth replaces fact in many of these instances. Driving at night should be avoided, otherwise normal precautions are fine. I expected it to take us until the end of the next week to make the US border.

It was my intention that we would enter the USA via Laredo and drive up to Dallas. From there we would continue across country to Flagstaff, Grand Canyon, Las Vegas and up to San Francisco. Who knows after that?

We drove from Guatemala City up to Huehuetenango, just thirty miles from the Mexican border. The drive to Huehuetenango was a very relaxed one hundred and eighty miles, however the road condition from twenty miles out of Guatemala City was really poor and just to test my flexibility my new found 'travelling companions' decided to see how my relationship counselling skills were. They fought from first light to early evening, with her threatening to walk off in the middle of a rather beautiful range of mountains because of some comment he supposedly made. She was definitely a fiery Costa Rican and it took almost half an hour to coax her back into his car for the remainder of the journey. How do I get into these things? Give me the Taliban any day!

The last fifty miles of Guatemala were mountainous and beautiful. The crossing into Mexico was unexpectedly straightforward with friendly, helpful officials. There was a spectacular gorge, narrow and very deep, with a river several hundred feet below on one side of the road and a dam created lake on the other. Unfortunately, as is often the case in these countries, the dam was classified as a military installation and photography was forbidden.

The two hundred mile drive to Tuxtla was hot, beautiful but relatively uneventful. My 'groupies' were keeping up with me and appeared to have called a truce, however I was not used to thinking for three. I am afraid Ted had no idea about travelling and had to ask advice on most things except food and drink.

I wanted to keep moving and set out early from Tuxtla for Oaxaca. Once again the whole journey was surrounded by lush green mountains. Many were clearly volcanic and the varying shapes made a fantastic vista. We were stopped by police a couple of times, including once at a roadside police station. As I pulled over to the side of the road for the officer to take a closer look at Bridget, I looked over to the building and realised it included a jail! The structure was literally a caged area measuring around eight feet by ten feet plus a covered area of approximately the same size that offered the prisoners shelter from the blazing sun, but it was an all metal building so the heat must have been awful. From what I could see, around a dozen inmates were housed in this structure. One prisoner noticed the car and suddenly all the inmates were hard up against the metal mesh of their 'cage'. I quickly discovered that at least two could speak English when they commented on the car. One asked if I would take him with me, but I replied, "You wouldn't all fit in the car." He said laughingly, "Never mind them, just take me."

Further on, during the early afternoon, a fuel tanker travelling towards me threw a stone into Bridget's windscreen causing a nasty crack. I would probably need to replace it in the States.

We arrived in Oaxaca around five o'clock and started looking for a hotel when I suddenly realised that Ted's Volvo was no longer behind me. Thinking that he had been stopped by the traffic lights I pulled into the side of the road and waited. After around ten minutes he still hadn't appeared so I walked back a little way but could see no sign of him. I didn't like to leave Bridget at the side of the road with all my belongings inside so I returned to the car and waited a further ten minutes before deciding that he must have turned off and was probably lost. I decided to continue on and find the Holiday Inn, which we had discussed staying at, and expected he would eventually do the same.

There was a week-long festival in Oaxaca so hotels were very full, but fortunately the Holiday Inn were able to give me a room and just after seven o'clock I went out for a meal. Sure enough, when I returned, the manager said that an American had turned up looking for me and that he thought they had gone to a restaurant next door. When I found them they looked none too pleased and it was not surprising, as it transpired that Ted's Volvo had caught fire and was completely burnt out at the side of the road. Lots of Mexicans in the area helped them get all their belongings out of the car and generally assisted, but the car was a total write-off. After some discussion over their options, they planned to fly on to the States from Oaxaca on the first available plane, but the episode must have been very frightening for them. All the excitement meant that I never got to see much of the city, which is rich in colonial architecture and archaeological sites.

The next morning I got back on the road, this time to Pachuca, which avoided going into Mexico City. The total distance we covered was four hundred and twenty-three miles including a ninety mile unscheduled detour (another wrong turn)! Although such a detour was inconvenient, it was made worthwhile by the stunning scenery. It also included driving down one of the steepest paved mountain roads that I have been on and it was exhilarating. However once I discovered we were going in the wrong direction, I realised that we would have to climb back up the same gradient. Bridget excelled again, not only taking the climb in her stride but also enduring the heat (mid thirties) and traffic. She had now motored at least seven hours a day for each of the last seven days and had two more to go before she would get a rest.

My error in navigation was discovered when I spoke to a policeman at one of the many road toll booths. He asked where I was going and pointed out that it would be quicker to go in the opposite direction. So I turned around to head back and the toll keeper wanted me to pay to go back through the gate. I felt that this was a shoddy way to treat a poor lost tourist who, after all, had only turned around and so, refused. We had a short stand-off before the rapidly lengthening queue of honking traffic persuaded him to waive the charge.

What should be the penultimate day in Mexico started well when we quickly found the road out of Pachuca, towards Cuidad Victoria. Often an hour can be wasted trying to find the correct highway out of town. The first fifty miles passed without incident and then we turned off the main highway, which went to Mexico City, and headed north. The scenery was stunning with huge mountains all around and I would happily nominate this route as the best MG driving route in the world, if only the authorities would remove the ridiculous speed humps in every village, often as many as twelve in a row. Considering the total lack of any roadworthiness requirements on the vehicles and the lack of police to enforce any sort of driving standards, I was at a loss to understand the reason for these irritating and damaging lumps of concrete.

The road surface itself was in reasonable condition for most of the route and the bends were beautifully banked, making cornering perfect. If the local authority could be persuaded to close the road to traffic for a day it would make the best possible one hundred and fifty mile MG race event.

However, with all the speed humps the first two hundred miles of our journey were painfully slow, taking almost five hours. Then, during the late afternoon, I thought Bridget was sounding rather hoarse and noticed the oil pressure was unusually low and the temperature high. I decided to stop and check the oil level, even though I had checked it before we left. Just as well I did because I found oil leaking profusely from the valve cover. When I removed the cover the gasket was in two pieces so I replaced it with a spare from the boot and restored the cover. Although that helped, the engine was missing at low revolutions and the tick over was poor. I would need to check the carburettor settings as I believed they were running too rich.

We only just made it to Ciudad Victoria before nightfall.

Our last complete day in Mexico was fairly straightforward, with Bridget running well as long as I kept the revs over two thousand five hundred. The temperature was well into the thirties but the road surface was smooth and so we made good time. We spent that night in Nuevo Laredo and I intended to get to the frontier with the USA early the next morning.

Exiting from Mexico was far easier and quicker than I had ever expected. In fact, I simply drove straight out without getting an exit stamp in my passport or anything, I just passed through the customs area and over the International Bridge to the US entry point. I am not at all sure if I was supposed to do that or if I accidentally short circuited the system but if all the signs are in Spanish and you don't understand the language, what can you do? They have probably listed me as an illegal immigrant by now!

# NORTH AMERICAS

*Location: USA and Canada*
*Timeline: 25th July 2009 to 25th September 2009*

I was pleasantly surprised at how quick and straightforward entering the States was by road. I had expected all sorts of paperwork and searches but again it was very easy, with the exception of purchasing car insurance. This did present some difficulties which took me several days to resolve. Each State has its own rules regarding auto insurance and in Texas insurance is compulsory, which is pretty much universal, but to purchase it you need to have a Texas residency. The only exception to this is a 'non residency' temporary policy, which in most cases requires your vehicle to be licensed in Mexico! When you turn up with a UK registered car and are touring the whole time it causes difficulties. I was only able to resolve the issues by using my hotel address, which is not strictly correct as that is also where the car is supposed to be garaged.

We made our way from the border to San Antonio, home to Davy Crockett, the Alamo and all that. Bridget's engine was still far from well and so I set about trying to resolve the problems. On inspecting the spark plugs I found them all covered with heavy carbon deposits, which suggested either poor ignition or the fuel being too rich. The latter is what I thought to be the problem. I removed the air filters and as I did I noticed that they were in poor condition and looked as if they had sucked in a lot of oil. This was probably caused when the gasket failed previously, so I decided they needed replacing. These I had to source directly from K & N as the local distributors didn't stock the correct ones for Bridget. I also adjusted the mixture control on both carburettors and would wait to see how things were driving to Dallas.

Driving conditions were now excellent, with no concerns about the road surface or general driving standards.

We left at eight o'clock under a cloudy sky, although the temperature remained in the ninety degrees Fahrenheit. I discovered again that the American oil companies have little trust in the honesty of their customers; a situation I personally find disreputable. If you wish to pay by credit card it has to be an American card with an American billing address, from which you have to supply the five digit zip code. If you have any other international card you have to take it into the cashier and she charges your card before you fill up, but that is not practical if you do not know precisely how much fuel you are going to take. The only alternative is to use cash.

Bridget ran well as long as I kept the engine revolutions below four thousands per minute, otherwise she started misfiring. When she ran at the lower revolutions she was very smooth. Next I would check all the fuel supply parts as this trouble was first noticed after filling up at a Mexican service station and we might well have got some dirt with it.

We had now completed thirty thousand miles and Bridget would soon require another service. I had sourced and fitted her new air filters and I would try to get some replacement points. Unfortunately, having tried to email three MG clubs in the southern states, we had no reply, so it would appear that where I had thought they would be as helpful as my friends in Australia, I was sadly mistaken. No matter, we ran from England to southern India with almost no help other than from the Maharana of Udaipur, so I was sure we could manage here.

Dallas, like most American cities, is very spread out, and using a car to go anywhere is the only real option. As someone who enjoys walking I found this a little irritating, particularly as they construct groups of hotels in the same area but there were few, if any, facilities within walking distance. It is the only country in the world that I have visited where this happens; even in Australia, where things have become decentralised, there are shops and restaurants around the hotels.

I decided to up-stakes and move on a day early from Dallas. I had removed Bridget's carburettors and there was indeed a great deal of dirt in one, which I was hoping was the cause of the trouble. Certainly her engine was sounding good whilst stationary and she ticked over beautifully, but the next day we would find out if that had cured the problem. We would be on the road to Amarillo; I could hear the song already!

It was the last day of July and the drive from Dallas to Amarillo went well. The first one hundred miles was a little worrying as I kept smelling petrol, a problem that I had experienced previously. Eventually I pulled into a service station and lifted the bonnet (I didn't want a repeat of the Volvo's fate). Instead of the trickle that had happened before, it was running out quite freely. I switched off the engine and removed the carburettor bowl, where the leak appeared to be. The gasket looked OK but I wasn't totally convinced and so I checked my stores for a spare. Unfortunately it was not one of the items that I had but I did have some 'instant gasket', which I used. I also refitted the old gasket and after that I had no further problem. The remainder of the journey was really straightforward.

As the day's drive was fairly short I started rather lackadaisically but Bridget was very ready to go. She accelerated smoothly and easily as I tried to detect any of her previous problems but we seemed to have, at last, cleared them. The air was cool and the sun bright when we left Amarillo but the temperature soon climbed as the miles slipped by.

With only about sixty miles to go I passed a white utility van at the side of the road and noticed the logo on its side, KRQE News 13. I watched it in the rear view mirror as it pulled out into the traffic lane and accelerated quickly. As it drew level I realised it was keeping pace with me so I looked over and sure enough the window was wound down and the driver was gesticulating. We pulled over onto the hard shoulder and the driver jumped out and came back to Bridget and me to introduce himself. His name was Ian Schwartz and he wanted to know "Are you really driving around the world?" So I told him about the adventure and we met up again in the late afternoon to record an interview. It all helped to spread the word.

Unfortunately, when I restarted Bridget after our encounter on the highway, the misfiring started again and she was losing petrol from one of her carburettors once more. It could have been temperature related so I decided to see how things were in the morning.

I removed and refitted the carburettor float chamber first thing and Bridget was as good as gold all day. The drive to Flagstaff was only just over three hundred miles but it was very hot again so I kept our speed down to around fifty-five mph. Several people along the way said they saw our television interview, which was nice to know.

The countryside was now taking on a new look with desert and mountains appearing. The desert here was different from those in Australia, Peru and Pakistan. It was populated with lots of small trees or bushes, I am not sure which, although I think some was tumbleweed, but they gave the landscape a speckled appearance. The hills that we first came across were in New Mexico and were bright red sandstone, similar in colour to the outback sand in North Queensland, Australia. As we passed the city of Gallup the colour changed to yellow. The shapes of these hills were typical of what I have seen as a youngster in cowboy films with steep cliffs and plateau tops. I was half expecting to see Tonto. Approaching Flagstaff, the first real mountains came into view, more ragged than those in the Himalayas or southern Andes.

Bridget celebrated her own special achievement on this day as we crossed the state line from New Mexico into Arizona; her odometer completed its first one hundred thousand miles and that evening displayed '000161'.

We left Flagstaff early in the morning and headed to the Grand Canyon's southern rim. This was the area most commonly visited although I was hoping to see the northern rim also. The morning was bright and soon became very hot. Bridget was running well again although we still had a problem at the higher revs.

It was only ninety miles to the canyon and what a spectacle it was. I had been prepared to be disappointed after all the other natural wonders that I had seen but the Grand Canyon is spectacular, whatever else one may have witnessed. It was not just its vastness, although that is impressive, but the size and shapes of all the hillocks, or whatever the correct name is, that are quite unique. I had been told you get a quite different perspective from the other rim and so I looked forward to that later in the week.

So what were my initial observations on the United States? It's funny how some of the things we observe are the most insignificant items. Clearly the significant items are geography, flora and fauna and culture, and these are unique in each part of the world. So it is extraordinary that two things I repeatedly noticed were the large number, and length, of the railway trains; and the whispering trucks.

Firstly, the trains, for those that do not know, are anything up to a mile or more in length with two, three or four engines pulling and/or pushing the wagons. 'Whispering trucks' is a reference to many of the large trucks, or rigs as they are known there, that make very little noise but just hiss slightly as they pass, even at speeds of seventy miles per hour. They were a terrific improvement over those in Central America that made an unholy din caused largely by poor maintenance.

As I say, the significant things are those given to us by nature and after Australia, South and Central America, I had noticed that there were considerably fewer birds in this part of North America and their colouring tends to be largely browns and black. The scenery I have already described, so that leaves the people.

Those I had met so far were just what I had expected from my previous visit to the States in 1980. They are outgoing, friendly, confident but also somewhat insular. Many had little understanding of what life outside of the US is like although they were more inquisitive than I previously found them. After a fairly slow start, they became aware of Bridget and the journey we were attempting and suddenly lots of offers to help were being received. Whether or not they would join in with some donations for UNICEF, remained to be seen. It occurred to me that if everyone who viewed the CNN IReport news item about us gave one dollar each, we would have reached our target right then.

From Grand Canyon we drove on to Page, a small town some ninety miles further north. Page, Arizona is a small and very young town. It really didn't exist until it was decided to build a dam, creating Lake Powell, and the town was officially incorporated in 1957. It also has a copper mine but the major income earner for the town today is tourism. It is a great jumping-off point for the Grand Canyon, both southern and northern rims, has a fascinating and quite unique canyon called Antelope Canyon and lots of water sports on the lake. The people are genuinely warm, hospitable and friendly, and they are also well aware of the outside world.

The owner of the local radio station, Dan Brown, a fellow MG owner (two in fact, a MGB and a TD), contacted me through our website and invited me here for a couple of days R & R. I thought this was very kind of him and that was before I knew that he had arranged a number of activities for my delectation. One in particular I want to say more about was a tour of the Antelope Canyon (or Slot Canyon as it is sometimes known due to its extremely narrow passage). The canyon was formed by flood waters and wind carving out the passageway in the red sandstone. With sunlight streaming in from the top, the walls, which are smooth but striped by different formation layers and shaped with wind carved undulations, have the effect of an artistic spectral design. During the afternoon I recorded an interview for the local radio station and then appeared at a local community event raising awareness and offering support to families affected by crime and drug abuse.

My second day in Page I worked on Bridget during the morning and cured the misfire at last. She still got a little hot and the carburettors were not perfect but we would continue the way we were. Late in the afternoon I was given the opportunity to try riding a Sea-Doo for the first time. I always knew these as water scooters and remember seeing one in a motorcycle shop when I was a mere slip of a lad. Since then I had always wanted to try one. My teacher, Janet, was marvellous and I had an absolute ball, even managing to show off and stand up on the seat whilst going full belt. Another ambition achieved.

We left on Thursday morning feeling considerably refreshed. I would recommend the resort of Page to anyone planning a trip to the Grand Canyon area as it offers so much more than just the canyon.

We ventured on towards Vegas and a last minute change of mind meant we did not go to the northern rim of the Grand Canyon, however we did pass through the Zion National Park which is another fabulous area of mountains and canyons. A second location on the trip well worth seeing is the Virgin River Canyon, once again dramatic, rugged sandstone cliffs and mountains with a good MG driving road. We arrived in Las Vegas at three o'clock and were now in our fourth state, having driven through Texas, Arizona, Utah and now Nevada.

Las Vegas is the city in the middle of a desert. Many people ask 'Why?' It was first established because water was available there. This served as a stopover for wagon trains and the railroad. In the early twentieth century it became famous for its speakeasies, mainly owned by different mafia gangs, which attracted tourists from around the US, but it was with the building of the Hoover Dam in 1930 that the population increased fivefold. With most of the new population being male labourers requiring some form of entertainment, Mormon financiers and the mafia developed the casinos and showgirl theatres. Today, it is a city for serious professional gamblers and for groups of twenty-something year olds on short fun vacations. I personally do not see it as a good venue for family holidays or romantic weekends. However, the American Broadcasting Company, ABC TV, gave us some excellent coverage on their news channel and helped raise awareness of UNICEF's work.

After three day's rest we drove out of Vegas early on Sunday morning and made good time driving north towards Carson City and Reno. After around eighty miles we turned left, heading for Death Valley National Park. This is one of the iconic drives in the USA that motor-heads must do, similar to the historic Route 66. It is supposed to be one of the hottest areas to drive in although I had some doubts about that after being in Pakistan and Australia.

Bridget started out well with no misfire or hesitation. Approaching the turn to Death Valley I thought I had fluffed the gear change when there was a grinding of gear cogs, but then I found it extremely difficult to shift into any gear. I pulled over and sprung the bonnet catch. Getting out and lifting the bonnet, I removed the top of the clutch master cylinder. Sure enough it was almost empty. When on earth did I last check the level? Apologising profusely to Bridget for such behaviour I fetched the clutch fluid from the boot and topped up the cylinder. I crossed my fingers hoping it would not require bleeding. However, it became obvious that it would need to be bled but I hoped we could at least get to San Francisco before having to do it.

We passed the original Nevada desert nuclear testing site and the morning's temperature was rising. Bridget's temperature gauge started climbing and whenever there was an incline the needle was going into the red. Not being able to change gear easily was making things even more difficult. As we passed Bad Water, a huge salt lake, there was a signpost warning of 'Extreme Heat for the next twenty miles'. It was not an exaggeration and to make things a little more difficult we had to climb a couple of thousand feet before dropping down the other side and then doing it all over again.

Halfway along this road there is a water stop, comprising of public toilets and a water supply for radiators but not for drinking. I decided to stop in the shade of a tree and allow Bridget's engine to recover.

There was an old Ford camper van already there and the occupants where a young couple from Torbay in the UK, who were motoring around the states for six months. With their assistance I tried a quick fix bleeding of the clutch master cylinder, which didn't work very well, but improved things enough for me to decide to continue to San Francisco. Bridget would be due another service there and I would fix the clutch at the same time.

Death Valley lived up to its reputation as being extremely hot and Bridget's engine was at the very maximum of her temperature range several times. I had to nurse her up the hills in third gear which helped bring the temperature down just enough to continue but it was touch and go. Several miles further on we drove through Kern River Canyon which is stunningly beautiful. The mountains tower over both sides of the cool, refreshing river as it meanders down the canyon floor with stretches of white water. We arrived in Bakersfield at five o'clock and would strike out for San Francisco the next morning.

The drive to San Francisco was interesting in that it meant driving through the American Fruitbowl area. This is just mile after mile, of apple, orange and lemon trees. There are vast areas of grape vines, evidence of California's wine industry, and also large areas producing almonds. Road and weather conditions were good and Bridget ran reasonably, with her gearbox almost back to normal. We arrived into 'Frisco' at three o'clock in the afternoon.

My first impressions were that this could be a fun city and that is what I found to be the case. There are the famous names such as Alcatraz, Fisherman's Wharf and the Golden Gate Bridge and it has more than its share of 'characters'. I made contact with the North California MG Owner's Club and immediately received an invitation to dinner by a couple who are members and were planning a trip in their MG to Europe. Craig and Kim supplied wonderful hospitality as well as helping me out by changing Bridget's oil which, because of disposal, is always a potential problem for me.

Whilst driving over to their home I was on highway CA-24 and became aware of a white saloon keeping pace beside me. I looked over expecting the usual photo opportunity and saw two lads in the front and a girl in the back. They waved to me, which I happily returned. and then without warning the girl 'flashed' me. I know our news coverage had referred to our drive as a 'global challenge' but that was not quite what they meant. However, I was warming to this city very rapidly.

Bridget now had fresh oil, new spark plugs and all the fluid levels had been checked. The clutch appeared fine and I had readjusted the carburettors because she was misfiring slightly. On Sunday we would start the trip north to Canada. I was reconsidering the route from Winnipeg as I was now back on time and might go to Chicago then onto New York and ship Bridget home from there, or possibly stay in Canada and drive over to Toronto. I would just have to see what took my fancy.

I chose to drive north from San Francisco on Highway US101, rather than the quicker route I-5, after several people told me that the coastal road was really pretty. I left immediately after an early breakfast; the weather was sunny but the temperature only just over seventy degrees Fahrenheit. Being a Sunday, the traffic was light.

The forty mile stretch of the US101 between Garberville and Pepperwood is called Redwood Highway or the Avenue of the Giants, referring to the giant redwood trees that are reputedly the largest in the world. I drove Bridget through the Chandelier Tree, which is one of four that have had a small roadway bored through the trunk. Not surprisingly they are big tourist attractions but fortunately the conservationists have ensured that no more suffer this fate in the future.

The drive as far as the town of Fortuna, eight miles north of the world's largest timber saw mill, was picturesque and I decided to stop there for the day as I had plenty of time to get to the Canadian border and I wanted to experience some of 'small town' America.

The next morning was decidedly chilly but sunny. We rejoined the

US101 north. We could either drive all day, making Portland by early evening, or take it easy and get there in another two days. Not being pressed for time, the latter was most likely and as the day progressed I decided to slow things down a little and enjoy the scenery. The road was still flanked by Redwood firs and then it met with the Pacific. The rollers were rushing up the beach and there was a multitude of rocky outcrops from twenty yards to a mile from shore. Sometimes we were at sea level with warning signs telling us we were in tsunami danger areas, and at others the road was several hundred feet above the beaches.

We crossed the state line from California into Oregon.

Driving through the Samuel H. Boardman State Park I saw a lay-by and pulled in. There was a trail sign-posted 'To the Bridge View'. I followed the trail and found that the road I had been travelling on was about to pass over a bridge several hundred feet high, although when on the highway it was impossible to see the structure. I managed to snap a shot of the bridge, but instead of returning to the car decided to continue walking and with some physical agility found a ledge that looked back across the bay and beach of the park. This view was many times more beautiful than the bridge.

We stopped for the day at Coos Bay, a small coastal town.

The last day on Route 101 was again scenic, warm and varied. The traffic was a little heavier than we been accustomed to recently but it was only noticeable because there were several stretches of single carriageway where overtaking was not possible. Bridget was fine although still suffering some misfiring.

Once again I took a gentle stroll amongst some of the Redwoods and found a pleasant spot overlooking Tankenitch Lake. It was beautiful, peaceful and felt remote, although it was not far off the highway. We arrived in Portland shortly after lunch. I had not been there since 1980, just before Mount St. Helens erupted and tore half the mountain away, and my memories of it were not particularly delightful. However, is has undergone considerable regeneration and is now a vibrant pleasant place to be. Moreover, although it has more car parks than you could wave a big stick at, it is a city where people actually walk. I thoroughly enjoyed it.

The next day was to be my last day in the USA. We would drive up to Seattle ready to cross into Canada on Thursday. I had changed my mind about returning to Chicago to ship back to the UK and instead would drive to Toronto and return from there. My apologies to those in Chicago who were hoping we would call in.

Our last night in the US was in fact spent at Everett, just north of Seattle. The two hundred mile drive was easy and Bridget ran well with little misfiring. From here we would go to Vancouver where the local MG club was organising something and then I had a five day route across the Rockies planned out before going on to Calgary. Canada, I hoped, would be a lot of fun.

Then again, it's never over till the fat lady sings. Bridget's fuel pump failed and it proved difficult to change because of my location. I managed to persuade a company to let me use their hoist to get at the pump but we couldn't do the job that evening. It resulted in having to spend Thursday in Everett to complete the job, but this may have been part of the cause of her misfiring, she was suffering from fuel starvation.

We crossed the border into Canada just after lunch on the 21$^{st}$ August having replaced Bridget's fuel pump. She was still misfiring at low revs and at over four thousand revs per minute, but otherwise was running OK. I still believed the carburettors were not balanced.

We had been invited to stay with Peter and Anne Tilbury from the Canadian Classic MG Car Club and their home was only three miles from the USA border. Peter came down the drive to greet us and guide Bridget into a waiting garage. After the introductions we were joined by Rod Taylor-Gregg, a long time friend of Peter's and another MG owner to boot. We set about trying to resolve Bridget's misfire. Rod examined the jets and needles in the carburettors and noted that the jet of the rear 'carb' was somewhat higher than that of the front one. This meant that the starting position for the mixture control adjuster would be different, something that you would not be aware of if you just tried to balance them without first looking inside. After setting them up and tuning the mixture and idling adjusters, Rod and Peter soon had Bridget's engine running far smoother with only a slight hesitation between two thousand and two thousand five hundred revolutions. She would be alright for Sunday's slalom!

The club, jointly with the Canadian XK Jaguar Register, had a slalom event arranged for Sunday and Bridget and I had been entered.

We duly presented ourselves to the scrutineers to be inspected and then were introduced to the other club members and competitors. Bridget and I had never done one of these events before and were somewhat nervous, but the others made us feel at home. I had been promised that there would be no other Midgets and therefore Bridget would win her class, however that transpired to be slightly inaccurate. We had to drive three times around a track marked out with traffic cones (all the same colour), each lap taking a slightly different route, and this was against the clock. We made four attempts and our best time was forty-nine seconds. Needless to say we were not the fastest, but neither were we the slowest. The whole thing was great fun and we will certainly do some more of these events, but where the track doesn't favour left-hand drive cars!

When we got back to Peter's house I decided to check the spark plugs as I felt they must have been somewhat abused during the previous few weeks with all the misfiring, even though they had been replaced only six thousand miles earlier. We found that the gap on one of the plugs was almost non-existent and I chose to replace them all. The next morning we took Bridget to get replacement tyres and she ran without any hesitation or misfire whatsoever, so hopefully that would no longer be an issue. How many times have I thought that? A local dealer fitted four new tyres, replacing three that were on the edge of legality and one that was more than three quarters worn. Three of the five tyres I had were originally on the car when I bought her and had driven over forty eight thousand miles.

We said our farewells to Peter and Anne, and the others that we had so briefly met in Vancouver, and set course for Kelowna. We left at midday and the temperature was in the mid seventies. The road was smooth and Bridget was running really well. We would spend the next few days in the Rocky Mountains, the last of the three major mountain ranges on my journey, which I had yet to see. I had been told that Kelowna was the jumping-off point and that there was nothing much to see on the drive there. Nonetheless, I found the scenery beautiful with huge tree covered mountains interspersed with bare, rocky mountains and the occasional lake. The trees are mainly spruce and some appear precariously perched on the rocky faces of the mountains with little soil in which to put down roots.

We arrived at our destination at five o'clock and checked into a hotel. Kelowna is a tourist resort on the banks of Okanagan Lake. It appeared lively and still very busy even though school holidays were over. It was the starting point of my Rocky Mountain adventure.

My first impressions of Canada were overwhelmingly focused on the people, who were not only warm, friendly and hospitable but also very law abiding. The only other nationality I can think of similar to them is the Swiss. With regards to traffic they rarely speed, are patient, courteous, obey traffic signals and give way to queue jumpers, pedestrians and MGs.

From Kelowna we headed south on Highway 3B towards Rock Creek and Kettle Valley. The whole area is overshadowed by fir tree forested mountains. Occasional rivers and creeks are seen flowing mellifluously over gravel beds and rocks worn smooth by the flow. I had decided to stop by one of these rivers, between Carmi and Rhone, to take some photos of Bridget and the scenery, when I spotted a helicopter carrying a very large box object under it. The chopper was skilfully manoeuvred between the hundreds of fir trees so that the box could be emptied by ground crew and then it departed the way it had come. The pilot could not have had more than a few feet in which to manoeuvre its rotors and it was fascinating to watch.

We spent the night at Nelson, a town on the banks of Lake Kootenay, British Colombia. Just like Kelowna the night before, Nelson is a tourist trap.

The following morning we headed north to the town of Proctor where we caught the longest free ferry in the world, across Lake Kootenay. Then we joined Highway 3A north to Creston. This town had been in the news recently due to the purported behaviour of some polygamous sects. Outwardly it is just like many small towns in this part of British Colombia, a community with friendly, helpful people in a pretty location, and I am sure that most of them are just that. The scenery in this area is wonderful and there are a lot of Bavarian immigrant families here.

Whilst driving at around sixty-five mph just north of Creston, the River Moyie flowing on our right, I spotted something in the river. At first I thought it was a bear, so I braked hard, turned one hundred and eighty degrees and returned to the spot where I first saw the creature. I jumped out of the car, crossed the road and also a railway line. I followed the bank along until I spotted the animal again but it turned out to be a moose. It had only one antler and was apparently cooling off in the river. I took several photos before starting back to Bridget. Then I noticed a heron stalking some sort of delicacy down the river so I managed to snap some extra footage.

That night we would stay in Kimberly and I had decided not to drive the following day but to go walking around some of the forest trails before continuing to Calgary.

What a good decision it turned out to be. I spent six hours walking around the Kimberley Nature Park hoping to see some black bears, deer and perhaps a cougar. Instead of bears I found mosquitoes which attacked me unrelentingly for much of the day. I was trained in unarmed combat so when I caught two aggressively gnawing at my leg I despatched them both with a chop to the back of the neck. Don't tell me the day of the Great White Hunter is over! My legs would no doubt ache tomorrow as it was the first reasonable exercise I had had for some time but it was worth it. I didn't see another soul the whole time I was out there and it was so peaceful. Next time I must remember to give myself a swift squirt with the Bushman's. A little reluctantly we left Kimberley, where I would have liked to have done some more walking, but I had promised to be in Calgary that evening.

The first part of the drive was pleasant with pretty scenery, bright sunshine and Bridget running smoothly. We stopped at Colombia Lake just past Canal Flats and a huge timber mill. The view over the lake was beautiful and the colour of the water a perfect Royal Blue.

At the town of Radium Hot Springs we turned right picking up Highway 93 and entering the Kootenay National Park. I was back to one of my two favourite areas of nature: serious mountain country. The scenery was magnificent, with towering craggy mountains partly covered in pines and firs, raging rivers, trickling streams and some mountains with snow still on the peaks. On one stretch of road there was a sign 'Wolf on road, DO NOT STOP'. A little further on I spotted a deer and so had to stop. I couldn't miss the opportunity of snapping a deer even if there was a wolf about, but I saw no sign of it. On the other side of the Kootenay National Park is Banff and another park with more majestic mountains. It really is a fantastic part of the world.

The drive to Calgary should have only taken four to five hours. With all the stops I wanted to make it took me just over seven hours. That was the last major mountain range of the trip and I really will have to revisit them all again and spend far more time walking.

Calgary, situated to the east of the Rocky Mountains, is home to some one million people. It is twinned with, amongst others, the city of Jaipur, or the Pink City as it is sometimes called (see page 47). We were to stay here for two and a half days and the Calgary MG Car Club entertained me magnificently. They were assisted on Saturday by the Vintage Sports Car Club when I was taken on a garage tour to see a number of cars and motorcycles in various stages of renovation. In the afternoon I was taken to experience the Calgary Highland Games in High River, where a number of ex-pats threw hammers and tossed cabers, but they were even worse shots than the Taliban, so I stayed. There was also a pipe band competition that I thoroughly enjoyed and the Scotch Pies were excellent. On Sunday we went up to Bragg Creek and the scenery is gorgeous, with mountains as a backdrop to the creek and waterfalls.

Our departure came all too quickly and we had to move on Monday morning towards Medicine Hat. We had been invited to stay at the Callaghan Hotel and Convention Centre and asked to do a couple of interviews with the local TV station and newspaper. As a bonus I found that the hotel and attached nightclub is frequented by many British servicemen who train at a nearby location leased to the MOD for such purposes. I hadn't expected to meet up with so many of my fellow countrymen in that location.

Next day we were off to Regina en route to Winnipeg. Bridget was running so well it was almost becoming boring. Admittedly we had to change the brake light switch in Calgary, a replacement being supplied by Bob and Resa, members of Calgary MG car club. They actually took the switch off their own MGB. Quietly I was pleased with Bridget, as it was really nice to motor along without having to constantly scan the instruments for signs of trouble and keep listening to the engine beat.

We stopped for a few moments for a photo shoot at the Saami Tepee, which is the worlds tallest tepee. This is a tourist attraction in Medicine Hat that was originally constructed in Calgary for the Olympic Games.

From there we continued along Highway 1 East towards Regina. The landscape now changed dramatically and I was faced with the wheat growing plains of Canada. Here were thousands of square miles of cereal growing land, water holes with wildfowl, bison herds, domestic animals and salt flats. They say, a little cruelly, when talking of this area of Canada, "If your dog runs away, you can still see him a week later."

We arrived in Regina a little after lunch and having checked into the hotel I went for a walk over to the local shopping mall to buy something to drink. I had only just entered the mall car park when two guys jumped out from behind a drive-in something or other, one carrying a camera on his shoulder and the other a microphone. They asked "Do you think the use of mobile phones should be banned when driving a car?" I wanted to answer, "Yes, because it can cause you to spill your whisky," but thought better of it. The state was considering making it illegal to drive and use your phone and the local TV station was getting the publics view. When we finished the poll item I explained what I was doing in town and the news editor of CBC asked to do another interview the next day about our adventure. So we were going to be delayed the next morning whilst they filmed Bridget.

Following the interview with CBC, first thing in the morning, we set off for Winnipeg, a distance of some three hundred and ninety miles. I had checked Bridget's oil level and added some brake fluid to the master cylinder. During the run I checked the fuel consumption and even though our average speed had increased to sixty mph, consumption had improved to thirty-four miles per gallon. Bridget really was a delight to drive.

Winnipeg is a pleasant city with lots of recreational areas. It's very pedestrian and cyclist friendly, something I have noted in several locations in Canada, probably more so than any other country we had visited. However, the countryside for hundreds of miles around is very flat and lacks the pleasing vista that hills and mountains give. I must also mention the trains that I saw several times, which are in another league altogether to those I had seen in the States. I measured one as I passed, it being stationary at a red light, and it was two miles long! It consisted of around two hundred wheat filled wagons.

I had a bad night's sleep. For some reason my body had broken out in a series of heat bumps. They covered my head, neck, arms and legs and they itched like mad. Having been awake all night, I was not really in good condition for the day's drive ahead of me.

We left at half past seven in the morning, before the sun got up. The temperature overnight had caused a light dew and was a very welcome break for me. The heat bumps did not itch if they were kept cool, so at least the first phase of the drive should be OK.

We took Highway 1 east from Winnipeg and eventually joined Highway 17 to Thunder Bay. The scenery was an improvement over the previous drive, with pines and even small hills breaking up the horizon. Then we arrived into Lakeland, where there are hundreds if not thousands of lakes everywhere. I would have loved to have found one of the 'glassy' ones to park Bridget beside and take a photograph of her and her reflection but it was not possible to get close enough.

During the day we stopped at Longbow Lake to refuel and Carlton Dent, owner of the service station, overhearing what I was telling an inquisitive passer-by about our adventure, said the fuel was on him as his donation to the UNICEF fund. I was thrilled that someone with so little information about our adventure would put his hand so deep into his pocket to support us.

The day's drive was a little less than five hundred miles and Bridget seemed as fresh when we arrived as she was at the start. She was certainly running as well as she had ever done since I bought her.

Ten miles short of our destination we crossed a bridge over the Kaministiquia River. I looked to my left and realised from the view that there was a fairly substantial waterfall. It transpired that it was the Kakabeka Falls, which are just beautiful.

When we arrived in Thunder Bay I found a high pressure hose car wash and cleaned off all the dust that had accumulated over the past ten days. We received an e-mail from New Zealand requesting a radio interview about the journey, which was nice as we hadn't even been there. Bridget was becoming an international star!

My heat bumps were just too much and I decided after another bad night that I was not in a fit state to drive. I thought if I had one day in the hotel, which was air conditioned and cool, that my body would recover. I caught up on my e-mails, magazine articles and general administration.

Sunday morning and I felt as if I was a day late and had to keep reminding myself, "A day late for what?" On top of that my phone alarm was an hour late so instead of getting up at six o'clock it was seven o'clock. Still, it was a misty morning again and when we left Thunder Bay it was cool. My body seemed to have responded to the day's rest and Bridget appeared to be performing well. I did not set a specific location to reach that day so I wouldn't be disappointed.

The scenery was improving all the time. The pine forests spread out on both sides and as we drove through MacKenzie I got my first good look at Lake Superior. It was much the same as looking out to sea but you need to remember this is a fresh water lake. Bridget was still consistently getting attention as we made our way along the highway and we were constantly approached by curious strangers at service stations and viewpoints.

I decided to stop for the night at Sault Sainte Marie, after some four hundred and fifty miles. This put us two days from Ottawa and I had now been contacted by the local MG club there. I promised we would let them know where we were staying and for how long. I also made contact with Mediaworks, New Zealand, owners of a number of radio stations who had asked to do a telephone interview, and told them of our schedule.

Our next destination en route was North Bay. The road followed the north coast of Lake Superior through the towns of Marathon and Wawa, and Pukaskwa National Park. The scenery now was breathtaking as some of the trees had started to turn colour so that in addition to green, there were now yellow, gold, orange and red leaves.

From North Bay we drove on to Ottawa, arriving so quickly I was taken by surprise. The countryside on this leg of the journey was far more agricultural and less forested. Nonetheless, I saw an antelope of some description making its way through a wheat field but it was too far away to get a photograph.

Bridget was still running so consistently well that I was concerned in case I forgot my recently acquired mechanical knowledge. Checks over the last three days showed that we were still averaging sixty mph and her overall fuel consumption was thirty-four miles to the gallon.

I spent the afternoon catching up with my administration and e-mails and in the evening I was entertained by the Ottawa Austin Healey Car Club. They are a good crew and as usual had a mixture of cars with many owners having MGs as well as Healeys. This raises the conundrum of whether they are MGers or in fact Austin Healey people.

The city of Ottawa is of course the country's capital and there are a number of interesting historical Parliamentary buildings. It is a pleasant city which you can walk around easily and also has a good public transport system.

In the evening of day two around a dozen members of the Ottawa MG Car Club gathered in the hotel and we commandeered the lounge for an impromptu MG meeting. It was all very convivial but we had to conclude early as I was scheduled to do the radio interview. However, I must mention one special friend that Bridget made during this visit. Polly Blue is an MGB that drives Trish Adams around Ottawa, and all over Canada, and she and Bridget hit it off immediately. They have been regularly e-mailing each other ever since.

There was now only one thousand miles left to drive before arriving at Halifax from where we would ship Bridget home to England, and I was struggling with the idea that it was almost over. Nevertheless, I still had Montreal, Quebec and Nova Scotia to look forward to en route.

We had left Ottawa just after nine o'clock in the morning and found Highway 20 East easily. The drive was uneventful except for the usual waving, horn tooting fans. We completed the near two hundred miles in three hours, arriving in time for lunch. Bridget was still running well.

It will be immediately apparent to anyone who has travelled anywhere in Canada that the city of Quebec is different. Regular readers of my website will have already deduced that I am not really a city person and as we approached the end of this journey my patience with city ways was diminishing. Quebec changed all that and I quickly realised what I had been missing for much of the second half of this adventure; history.

One of the few figures I learnt about in school, and remembered, was General James Wolfe and he is one of several characters I had always felt akin to in that he attempted tasks that others felt were unlikely to succeed just because they were difficult. I can't say much more as my cousin who lives in France has forbidden me from making any disparaging remarks surrounding events from the campaigns of 1759, or any similar subjects, but the city of Quebec is inextricably linked with Wolfe.

The central area of Quebec is easily accessible on foot. The hotels have a feel about them that is different to most other locations in the Americas. The architecture is obviously, and some might think overly, European, but it gives an atmosphere to the city that is lacking in most others. Unlike Ottawa, which I enjoyed, Quebec is not a major shopping experience. The big fashion houses are not present pushing their latest design, which is not to say that Quebec doesn't have good shops, it does, but they are not displayed as a major event in life. Quality of life is more important, with food and drink being the major players, along with music, the arts and historical interest. Certainly tourism is a major contributor to the city's coffers, but it is achieved with class. You can also get a reasonably good beer in Quebec!

Our second day in Quebec brought with it the first rain we had

had since the deluge in Panama City. The temperature was noticeably lower and I wondered if this marked the official end to Canada's summer. The next day we would leave Quebec on the last part of our journey through the North Americas. We were going to go to the northern part of the province then around New Brunswick and Nova Scotia before entering Halifax to prepare to return home.

We left Quebec early and took route TC-20 following the St Lawrence River north and east. The scenery improved with every mile covered. The trees were really colourful in places although many still had their summer coverage. Once again I kept a keen vigil for elk, moose and bears, and once again saw none. I did see plenty of seals sunbathing on rocks just off the beaches. Once we were past Saint Maxime du Mont Louis we turned right and headed into the mountains around Murdochville.

Now we were back to the elementary pleasures of beautiful forested mountains, fast moving rivers and deep opal coloured lakes. I have to add though that we also discovered the worst road surfaces in all of Canada and the USA. Bridget coped well, but I would have to check her thoroughly to make sure nothing had shaken loose. I'm afraid her rear licence plate had fallen victim to a steep slope again and the fixing screw that Peter Tilbury so kindly replaced in Vancouver was lost. I would have to do a temporary repair with an electrical tie once more.

Several people had mentioned the town of Gaspe as a possible stopover, given my propensity to look for animals. There are purported to be many in this area plus the opportunity to go whale watching. I decided to splash out the dollars and took a boat out into Gaspe Bay and if necessary into the Gulf of St Lawrence. The trip normally lasts around two and a half hours. Everything started well, on time and with an excellent guide who explained which whales were in the area and their habits, and what we might expect to see. He overlooked mentioning the plunging temperature and rain.

We quickly came across a pod of dolphins as the boat ploughed steadily out into the bay. As we cleared the Cap-Gaspe headland the swell became noticeably more yawning, but then we spotted our first whales. They were minke, the second smallest variety, averaging only seven metres in length, but were fairly close to the craft. Shortly after this we found our first fin whale, also called the finback or razorback. This is the second largest mammal after the blue whale, which are also in these waters. I had always wanted to see a live blue whale since seeing the one in the Natural History Museum in London as a child, but this was not to be the day.

Suddenly disaster struck! I turned to get a snapshot of a fin whale blowing when a gust of wind whipped my blue MG cap from my head and I saw it flying through the air several metres from the boat. We heard, on returning to port in the afternoon, that a whale with a go faster stripe and blue MG cap was spotted cavorting around the bay but I think someone was having a laugh at my expense.

The sea then became more severe and the cold was really penetrating, even the icebergs were turning blue. We returned to the wharf at around half past twelve and it was three o'clock before I had thawed out, but it was well worth it. Bridget was refuelled, oiled and ready to go on to Fredericton, my one wish was that the road condition would improve again.

The drive from Gaspe to Fredericton was as varied as it was beautiful. It started as a coastal drive then we turned inland through forests and hills with the resultant rivers and lakes. The trees generally still had some way to go before they gained their full autumnal foliage, but some had already changed colour and the mix was just sublime.

Fredericton is the capital city of New Brunswick. I had some difficulty getting accommodation as they were hosting a week long international jazz festival which is an annual event, but in spite of this, I eventually managed to find a room.

I sent an e-mail to David Nielsen, my contact at the Fredericton Area British Automobile Club, and within half an hour some dozen members who had been attending their monthly meeting arrived at the hotel to welcome me and chat about the trip. The following day I was treated to lunch by David and Jim Bleakney, then shown around the city before doing interviews with the Daily Gleaner, CBC Radio and CBC Television. Following a lovely dinner prepared for us by David's wife, Carolyn, Jim and his wife and daughter, Ellie and Jill, took me to a 'Shine and Show' meeting. All in all a very good day and I extend my hearty thanks to everyone that made my visit special.

After leaving Fredericton, Bridget and I drove the short distance to Moncton. It was looking most unlikely now that I would see any bears during my visit, which was a little disappointing. I did, however, see a couple of deer grazing at the side of the highway. The weather stayed fine until the evening when there were a couple of light showers, but the temperature had noticeably dropped from a week earlier. People were starting to talk about the onset of winter when cars like Bridget get put away until the spring, so our departure timing was probably about right.

Our last day of travelling started with the discovery of a crack in Bridget's windscreen. It was not the type caused by a stone but appeared more like a stress fracture; it would mean a replacement when we got back to Oxford. The list of things to be done was growing.

Arriving in Halifax, I went straight to another 'Show and Shine' meeting in the suburb of Bedford. I had been invited along by Bob Hamilton of the Halifax branch of BATANS, British Automobile Touring Association of Nova Scotia. It was a great way to meet some of the members and view some very nice cars, including an early 1960's Jensen, which is quite rare.

The following evening I was invited to spend some time telling the members about Bridget and our adventure, at the end of which they presented me with some lovely mementoes. They also made a very generous donation to the UNICEF fund.

On Wednesday I took Bridget to the container yard to be packed snugly in her container for the voyage back to England. I was returning on Friday 25th September and hoping to meet up with her again in Liverpool around the 7th October. It seemed funny not having a drive ahead of me the next day.

# RETURN TO BLIGHTY

*Location: United Kingdom*
*Timeline: 25th September 2009 – 16th October 2009*

Still not quite able to bring myself to face it, I flew back from Halifax, Nova Scotia to Heathrow, London on the 25$^{th}$ September. It was a surprisingly sunny and warm day for the time of year. Steven, my son, was waiting at the airport to meet me and take me the half hour drive home and Matilda, my youngest granddaughter, was in the car. However, as she was only six months old when I left home, she didn't know me. It took half that day to get her to start smiling at me.

The following morning I contacted the shipping agents in Essex to confirm when Bridget was due to arrive into Liverpool. I was told she should be there on 9$^{th}$ October but this subsequently slipped to the 12$^{th}$ October and it would be the 14$^{th}$ before I could collect her. Meanwhile, the paperwork was completed.

On the morning of the 14$^{th}$ I caught a train from Oxford to Liverpool and walked to the container yard, where I was reunited with her. She had suffered no misfortune during her sea voyage and started up without difficulty. It was great to be back behind the steering wheel again although the break had only been two weeks.

I eased her tentatively out into the British traffic for the first time in sixteen months and felt quite nervous in case we were involved in an accident so close to the end. From the Liverpool docks area we made our way out onto the M62 motorway, joining the M6 south and eventually, via the M42, onto the M40 and back to Oxford. The total journey was under heavily clouded skies but the threatened rain held off. The traffic seemed strangely aggressive after the politeness of the Canadian drivers.

The one hundred and eighty miles took just over three hours. Passing through Oxford meant that the full circle was complete but the official finish would not be until the Friday.

At a half past two on the afternoon of 16th October, I drove Bridget from our home in Oxfordshire to Kimber House in Abingdon, the spiritual home of MGs. There was a small but enthusiastic gathering waiting for us, including journalists, television reporters, officials from the MG Car Club, friends, family and well wishers. Even though I was just arriving back, amongst the cheers, congratulations and general back-slapping, I found my mind was wandering back to the mountains, deserts and wilderness areas that I had been through and thought again about the safety of my friends in Iran and Pakistan.

Kimber House is the headquarters of the MG Car Club and is set beside the historic Cemetery Gate through which MGs leaving the factory, passed. Bridget had started her life here and so it was fitting that she should return here from her historic journey. She is the only MG Midget to have circumnavigated the globe in a single journey, proving that these cars were built to contend with far more than people, including most MG enthusiasts, ever credited them with. She has passed into MG history certainly, and afforded me personally with the greatest adventure of my life, but not the last.

# STATISTICS

27 Countries
39,000 Driving miles
1230 Gallons petrol (Gas)
32 Miles per gallon (overall average)
16 Months
139 Destinations
136 Hotels, inns, motels, hostels
6 Tyres
8 Oil changes
1 Engine rebuild

# TEN MOST ASKED QUESTIONS

The following are the most common questions that I was asked. Some, such as the first, were not asked until Australia, where I fixed stickers to the bumpers stating 'Around the World Drive'. Sometimes the question was couched slightly differently, such as "How far have you gone so far?" because the people thought it might just be some sort of joke.

Some of the questions are very culturally sensitive and though common in some areas they would rarely, if ever, be asked in others as they would be considered very rude, for example question five was almost always one of the first asked in Iran, Pakistan and India, but not at all in Australia, the USA or Canada.

1. Are you really driving around the world?
2. Where did you start from?
3. Why are you doing it?
4. Are you alone, no partner or support vehicle?
5. How much is the car worth?
6. When did you start out?
7. Which is the best place you have visited?
8. How many tyres have you used?
9. How fast does the car go?
10. What is the fuel consumption like?